Dangerous Liaisons

Dangerous Liaisons:

The marriages and divorces of Marxism and Feminism

CINZIA ARRUZZA

prologue by
Penelope Duggan

Resistance Books
IIRE
MERLIN PRESS

Published in 2013
by Merlin Press Ltd
6 Crane Chambers
Crane St
Pontypool
NP4 6ND
Wales
www.merlinpress.co.uk

in association with Resistance Books and IIRE
www.resistancebooks.org
www.iire.org

Dangerous Liaisons is issue number 55
of the IIRE Notebooks for Study and Research

© Resistance Books and IIRE

Edited by Penelope Duggan and Terry Conway

ISBN 978-0-85036-644-0

Translated from the Italian by Marie Lagatta
and Dave Kellaway

Catalogue in publication data is available
from the British Library

Printed in the UK by Imprint Digital, Exeter

CONTENTS

CONTRIBUTORS

Author

Cinzia Arruzza is Assistant Professor of Philosophy at the New School for Social Research. She studied in Rome (Italy), Fribourg (Switzerland) and Bonn (Germany). She works on ancient philosophy, ancient political thought, Marxism and feminism. She is also an IIRE fellow and a socialist and feminist activist.

Editors

Terry Conway is on the editorial board of the British socialist magazine *Socialist Resistance* and of the on-line English language magazine *International Viewpoint*. She is also a lifelong feminist and activist in the LGBTQ movement.

Penelope Duggan is a Fellow of the International Institute for Research and Education in Amsterdam where she lectures on women and political organizing. Publications include Working Papers of the Institute (notably *The Feminist Challenge to Traditional Political Organising*) and, as editor, of *Women's Lives in the New Global Economy* (1992, with Heather Dashner) and of *Women's Liberation & Socialist Revolution : Documents of the Fourth International* (2011). She is the editor of the on-line English language magazine *International Viewpoint*.

In memory of Daniel Bensaïd, the last of the untimely

PROLOGUE

"This small book aims to be a short and accessible introduction to the question of the relationship between women's movements and social movements, and the relation between class and gender."

With this as her goal, Cinzia Arruzza devotes the first two chapters to a brief summary of some of the important historical experiences of the first and second wave feminist movements and their relationship to the workers' movement. She then turns her attention to sketching out in the latter two chapters an overview of the theoretical discussions that have existed within the women's movements since the 1970s on the interrelationship between women's oppression, and other oppressions, and class exploitation, notably within the capitalist system. A substantial body of work has tackled the questions dealt with here as Arruzza indicates, thus the bibliography for this English-language edition has been substantially increased to take account of publication in English on these questions. This includes both the discussion in Britain that has developed since the publication of Juliet Mitchell's 1966 article in *New Left Review* "The Longest Revolution" with other notable contributions such as *Beyond the Fragments* by Sheila Rowbotham, Lynne Segal and Hilary Wainwright calling for a broad unity of trade unionists, feminists and left political groups, the work of Selma James and Maria Rosa Dalla Costa on "wages for housework" and the corpus of US feminist theory which to a far greater extent than in Britain engaged in a discussion with the "French feminism" or "difference theory" of Luce Irigaray. A glossary of people, in particular those who have contributed to Marxist and feminist theory, mentioned in the book has also been added.

In Arruzza's final chapter she proposes the need for "developing an outlook that can make sense of intersections and decipher the complex relationship between the patriarchal holdovers that drift like homeless ghosts in the globalized capitalist world and the patriarchal structures that have, on the contrary, been integrated, used and transformed by capitalism [which] calls for a renewal of Marxism." As she says, "The point is not whether class comes before gender or gender before class, the point is rather how gender and class intertwine in capitalist production and power relations to give rise to a complex reality, and it makes little sense and is not very useful to attempt to reduce these to a simple formula."

These questions of the interrelationship between the specific oppression of women, as the second wave feminist movement correctly characterized it, and other oppressions and exploitations were a subject of great concern to sections of that movement in its initial stages, despite its portrayal all too often as a movement simply of white middle-class women only concerned with their own situation (and some of the notable seminal works were indeed limited to this perspective, such as Betty Friedan's *Feminine Mystique*). This preoccupation was particularly marked for the currents characterized as "socialist feminist" (in some countries, for example France, where social democratic Socialist Parties were in power the use of the word "socialist" was rejected in favour of "class struggle feminism"). In Britain this current was for a period particularly strong in organizational terms, holding national conferences of several thousand women, larger than the "national women's liberation conferences" themselves.

The primary concern of these currents was in fact to reach out to working-class women, whether through the trade unions or more directly, including by activity in working-class communities. Women's committees in trade unions raising both the situation of women as workers and concerns of women as women were one of the primary forms this took, most often at the initiative of women activists who were also involved in the structures of the women's movement. They were thus predominantly in unions organizing white-collar workers in offices, laboratories and schools. (In countries such as Britain, Ireland or Denmark these initiatives could also link up with an already-existing tradition of women's organization within the structured labour movement.) But it should not be forgotten that the Ford women machinists' equal pay strike of 1968 is one of the founding events of the British women's movement. The Grunwicks strike of Asian women workers in the 1970s was another notable event. The support organized by the miners' wives groups in the year-long British miners' strike of 1984-85 was another indication of how in practice links could be found and forged between the situation of women as women, as workers and as members of working-class communities united in a common struggle to preserve their livelihood. Similar significant strikes of women workers or with women's involvement in major working class struggles can of course be found throughout the world.

An important expression of this interrelatonship was the November 1979 demonstration in defence of the 1967 Abortion Act in Britain jointly called by the Trades Union Congress (representing at that point some 13 million workers in Britain) and the National Abortion Campaign, a campaigning structure initiated by the the women's movement and bringing together women's groups, trades unions from local to national level and left-wing political groups.

While this relationship was important for socialist feminists from the beginning, it bore particular fruit during the historic miners' strike in Britain. Women in mining communities began to organize in support of the strike and set up their own organization "Women against Pit Closures". Domestic labour was collectivized through strike centres, which provided food and often childcare while at the same time women participated in picket lines and in speaking at meetings all over the world in defence of their communities. Socialist feminists were prominent in miners' support groups up and down the country. Unfortunately the defeat of the miners' strike by Margaret Thatcher's Conservative, anti-union government was a defeat not only for the trade union movement in Britain as is generally recognized on the left but also for women's liberation – and particularly for the socialist feminist current.

The contribution of this current to the women's movement has tended to be forgotten and written out of history by a mainstream discourse that has transformed feminism into counting how many women break through the glass ceiling in various sectors of big business, mass media or parliamentary politics, or dismissed the feminist movement as anti-men extremists, responsible for undermining men and family life and thus provoking all manner of social ills. This obliteration of the class-orientated socialist feminist current has prevailed to the extent that younger generations of Marxist feminists quite often simply do not know that such a current existed and identify all aspects of activist, militant feminism, such as women-only meetings, with the current known as radical feminist.

Within the women's movement "women of colour" also insisted on the specificity of their situation as such, as well as women, as workers, as lesbians. The British group Southall Black Sisters was formed in 1979 and brought together women of Black and Asian backgrounds. As Jane Kelly pointed out in her 1992 article "Postmodernism and Feminism" in *International Marxist Review* No 14:

> Lastly the 1980s were marked by the challenge of black women to the white-dominated women's movement. Black feminists pointed out that on many issues their experiences differed from white women. These included the family, the workplace, welfare rights, men, motherhood, abortion, sexuality and, centrally, the state. Although black women had been organizing together since at least 1973, including in several important strikes, and the first black women's conference in Britain was held in 1979, it was in the 1980s that

their voice was at last heard. Black women were organized in caucuses within the Labour Movement, in campaigns against deportation, against religious fundamentalism, against racism and in many other ways. Central to the debate between black and white feminists has been the relation between race, gender and class and the relative weight of each. For example black women explained that sometimes they have to put aside a fight against sexism to fight with black men against racism; at other times the struggle against male domination is paramount. This, along with black women's understanding of the racist state, led a significant proportion of black women to socialist conclusions and put black women's organization at the forefront of anti-imperialist struggles such as the campaigns against war in the Gulf.

One example of how the women's movement responded to women's different experiences depending on their ethnic or national origin is in the evolution of the international campaign for women's reproductive rights. First called the International Campaign for Abortion Rights (ICAR) it then became ICASC (International Contraception, Abortion and Sterilization Campaign) to eventually become the Women's Global Network for Reproductive Rights. This change reflected how the understanding of women's concerns shifted from that of notably white women in Western Europe and North America demanding the right to abortion and contraception to the non-white populations in those countries, such as the Bangladeshi women in Britain used as unwitting guinea pigs for the injectable contraceptive Depo-Provera in the 1970s or the Black women whose main concern was to avoid forced sterilization, to that of women globally and the whole set of interrelated issued concerning reproduction and women's health.

In fact it could be argued that the insistence of the women's movement that the combinations of exploitations and oppressions that different women experienced – thus meaning that precisely there was not a "one size fits all" answer to women's oppression – opened the way to post-modernism's rejection of systems and collective identitites. This resulted in a complete abandoning (at the level of theoretical discourse and discussion) of the possibility of collective struggle around common demands.

This was a far cry from the early days of the British Women's Liberation Movement, which had hoped to unite all women around first four, then six, then seven demands:

Demands One – Four
Passed at the National WLM Conference, Skegness 1971

1. Equal Pay
2. Equal Educational and Job Opportunities
3. Free Contraception and Abortion on Demand
4. Free 24-hour Nurseries

Five and Six
Passed at the National WLM Conference, Edinburgh 1974

5. Legal and Financial Independence for All Women
6. The Right to a Self Defined Sexuality. An End to Discrimination Against Lesbians.
(In 1978 at the National WLM Conference, Birmingham, the first part of this demand was split off and put as a preface to all seven demands)

The Seventh Demand
Passed at the National WLM Conference, Birmingham 1978

7. Freedom for all women from intimidation by the threat or use of violence or sexual coercion regardless of marital status; and an end to the laws, assumptions and institutions which perpetuate male dominance and aggression to women.

The goal of this book is to look at new ways of integrating the ideas of multiple oppression and exploitations and identities into a more developed Marxist analysis of the social relations in capitalism, that is to integrate contradictions such as women's oppression and racial oppression into the Marxist analysis of class society and thus overcome the separation and hierarchization of oppressions of which many Marxist currents have been guilty.

As an activist, Arruzza's concern is to enable the struggles of feminist women to be an integral part of the action of the radical anti-capitalist left in practice, not to remain at the level of a theoretical development.

Important contributions to the theoretical task have been made by Marxist feminists of preceding generations who share Cinzia Arruzza's perspective such as Stephanie Coontz and Lidia Cirillo, and by others through their activist work. In a series of lectures given in the International Institute for Research and Education in the 1990s, using the concept of Marxism as an analysis of a set of moving contradictions, Coontz posited:

> the methods of Marxism allow for self-correction on this issue, enabling us to explore the origins of male dominance and racism and in so doing to reconceptualize class itself. It is not a question of adding gender analysis to class analysis, or even showing how they intersect, but of using gender (and race, though this point needs development in a further paper) to reach a deeper, more historical and more useful definition of class.

Lidia Cirillo's work started from the debate with the "differentialists" in the Italian women's movement, the work of Luce Irigaray and Julie Kristeva having had a broad impact within the Italian Communist Party (PCI) which was relayed to the broader movement. Cirillo points out in her "Feminism of the Anti-capitalist Left" (*International Viewpoint*, June 2007):

> feminism is always born and reborn on the left, alongside revolutionary, democratic or progressive tendencies: on the margins of the 1789 revolution, in the national revolutions of the first half of the 19th Century, within the movement for the abolition of slavery in the United States, alongside the

workers' movement, in the radicalization of the 1960s and 1970s, in the global justice movement....

In one discussion of difference theory published as "For another difference" in *International Viewpoint* she notes:

The Italian philosophy of gender difference is very much indebted to the ideas of Irigaray as is openly recognized because Irigaray provides the indispensable element of theory – the idea that there is an innate gender difference in thought which is a biological fact linked to the morphology of sex and women's specific sexuality. Without this key idea it is impossible to claim gender difference as a value, to adopt it as the 'simple' paradigm.

Traditional feminism – both the radical and Marxist varieties – has usually reacted to male chauvinist difference theory (theoretical male chauvinism is basically a theory of gender difference) by explaining the historical nature of gender difference. Against men who theorized the distinctness of women on the basis of biological existence itself, its savage naturalness, of women's inability to sublimate or transcend it, feminists responded by partly throwing back the accusations, exposing its deprecating and ideological character; explaining what was true in women's distinctness as a fruit of history, a history of women's oppression.

More culturally aware feminists have never theorized equality in terms of uniformity. This identification is typical of reactionary and conservative thought and is nothing to do with Marxist criticism of the abstract equality embedded in bourgeois laws. The theory of gender difference mixes up the two separate approaches because its ideas have come out of contradictory and diverse political and cultural realities. The better tradition of feminism could not theorize gender difference as a value for a very good reason: gender difference, which coincides with history in the case of women, is oppression and consequently one cannot idealize it or identify with it.

Alongside this more abstract theoretical work, Heather Dashner, in a remarkable article "Feminism to the tune of the cumbia, corrido, tango, cueca, samba..." published in *International Marxist Review* in 1987, explored the process of radicalization of women in a series of Latin America countries after travelling to and meeting with the women involved, and showed how in practice the intersection of different identities (as women, as inhabitants of the *barrios* or *favelas*, as peasants, as workers in the informal sector, as mothers) could combine without any individual having to choose one identity over another as a "priority".

She expresses it thus:

In order to successfully deal with the contradictions between the traditional role society imposes on women and their new experiences gained through struggle itself, women have to be able to break the confines of the old social role and create a new one. This cannot be done by simply moulding the old accepted social role to include new behaviour patterns or practices: that, in any case, would be the bourgeoisie's answer. In a liberation perspective, the contradictions can only be overcome by creating a new concept and practice of women's role in society. In political terms, this needs to be expressed by clear demands and proposals which deal not only with general class questions, but also with specific women's questions.

In order for this to be possible, we have to be clear on the need for the existence of a clearly feminist pole within the women's movement. In practical terms, it has been shown that this need is felt by natural leaders who spring up in the survival and democratic women's movement. When they begin to confront their contradictions as women, they often seek out feminists to be able to talk over and understand what is happening to them. (...) What is needed, then, is to win these women to feminism and create a vanguard of the women's movement capable of correctly posing the fusion of general and specific demands in order to permit the emergence of a movement for women's liberation which in turn can influence all of the social movements.

It is with already existing work such as this that Arruzza can move forward with the shared project of working out "how class and gender can be combined together in a political project able to take action avoiding two specular dangers: the temptation of mashing the two realities together, making gender a class or class a gender, and the temptation to pulverize power relations and exploitative relations to see nothing but a series of single oppressions lined up beside each other and reluctant to be included within a comprehensive liberation project."

For all those of us either still or becoming involved in radical anti-capitalist political activity, within which we want to overcome the contradictions in ourselves and in how we express our own interests – that is, what we are fighting for as women – contributions such as Arruzza's, which give us the tools to understand the dynamics at work in that "social camp" which should be ours, so that we can claim it fully, are indispensable.

Penelope Duggan
in collaboration with Terry Conway

November 2012

INTRODUCTION

The history of the relationship between the women's movement and the workers' movement has been littered with successful and failed alliances, open hostility, affection and disaffection. Born in the crucible of the bourgeois revolutions, feminism quickly came into contact with social mobilizations and revolutions. At different times these revolutions opened up a new democratic space which allowed women to win hitherto unknown rights such as intervening and actively participating in political life and public affairs. Within the cracks opened up in the frozen cap of a centuries-old oppression women learnt to organize as women and to fight independently for their emancipation. However this process has been contradictory. At times it has been met with undervaluation and a tepid response from the organizations of the traditional labour movement and the new left. Outcomes have been controversial, ranging from exhaustive attempts to maintain a difficult relationship to an outright divorce.

This complex dynamic has also been reflected in the field of theory. In responding to the problems rising from women's struggles and processes of subjectification, feminist thinkers have given very divergent answers to the questions of the relationship between gender and class or between patriarchy and capitalism. There have been attempts to interpret gender through the methods of critical political economy, making gender oppression an extension of the exploitative relationship between capital and labour power or even to see male/female relations in terms of class antagonisms. Conversely some have argued for the priority of patriarchal oppression over capitalist exploitation. Theorists have tried to interpret the relationship between patriarchy and capitalism either as interplay between two autonomous systems or on the other hand to show how capitalism has taken on and profoundly modified patriarchal oppression.

The aim of this modest volume is to be a brief and accessible introduction to the issues of the relationship between the women's movement and labour and social movements and of the links between gender and class. In the first two chapters, we have summarized some of the historical experiences that have been important either in the process of women's organization and emancipation or in the linking up (or confrontation) of this process with the workers' movement. The last two chapters provide a brief panorama of the theoretical debate about the relationship between sexual/gender oppression and exploitation. It is an attempt to highlight the problems raised by the various conceptual frameworks. These problems still remain unresolved today. Neither the historical nor the theoretical sections of this book claim to provide a comprehensive reconstruction of the historical events or theoretical debates. I simply aim to put forward some examples and a way of accessing an extremely complicated and still open question. It is not an impartial reconstruction. Indeed, I base myself on some theoretical positions and some aims.

The first is that more than ever today it is urgent to work out theoretically the relationship between gender oppression and exploitation and especially the way in which capitalism has integrated and profoundly modified patriarchal structures. On the one hand, women's oppression is a structural element of the division of labour and therefore is one of the direct factors through which capitalism not only reinforces its domination in ideological terms but also continuously organizes the exploitation of living labour and its reproduction. On the other hand, the integration of patriarchal relations under capitalism has led to their deep going transformation – in the family, in terms of women's position in production, in sexual relations and with respect to sexual identity.

In order to understand these complex processes, it is absolutely vital to have a Marxism which really deals with the ongoing transformations and crises within a context where globalization is creating an increasingly feminized workforce and further changes in relations between men and women. Submerging gender into class and believing that freedom from exploitation automatically brings about women's liberation and the ending of sexual roles is a mistaken position. Equally wrong is to think that you can remove the class question by erecting ideological discourses that make gender the main enemy. What we need is to try and think through the complexity of capitalist society and its web of relations of exploitation, domination and oppression, avoiding unhelpful simplifications, however reassuring they might be.

My second theoretical position (and aim) is closely linked to the first one. As well as efforts at theoretical understanding, we must try to organize and politically intervene in order to bridge the gap between the feminist movement and the class struggle. We have to start by overcoming the old dialectic of priorities whereby dialogue and confrontation between the two sides has to be resolved either in asserting the priority of class over gender or vice-versa.

This is not only a theoretical question but also an organizational and political one. The way in which an understanding of the close connections between capitalism and women's oppression can lead to women becoming protagonists, able to build organizations and political arenas where women can feel at home, remains an open question. It can only be solved by real life practice and experimentation. However what we need right from the start is a willingness to go back to basics, not just in terms of theory but also organizationally and politically. Within our struggle for universal emancipation we need to open up a permanent laboratory of questioning and experimentation.

Cinzia Aruzza
2010

Chapter 1
MARRIAGES ...

1.1 Linking up the struggles

In 1844 Flora Tristan, with her book The *Workers' Union* in hand, decided to go on a long journey through the cities of France. She wanted to contact workers in meetings and taverns interested in listening to her ideas. In the book, published the year before, she had argued – some years before Marx and Engels – for the setting up of a workers' international which would unite all the world's workers.

A chapter in this book dealt with women's rights and examined the nature of the relationship between men and women inside the working-class family. Working-class women were humiliated, ill-treated, despised, physically abused, paid half the male salary and constrained to a brutal life of unending misery. The working-class woman was condemned to inferiority and irrelevance by a society that forced her into this role. Flora Tristan knew what she was talking about. Born in 1803 into a bourgeois family, fallen on hard times after the death of her father, she was obliged to marry the owner of the workshop where she worked as a dyer. She decided to finally leave her violent, heavy-drinking husband, whom she had never loved nor appreciated, when pregnant with her third child. She judged that being a pariah was better than being a slave. Between 1832 and 1834 she travelled through Latin America on a trip originally started as an attempt to recuperate part of her inheritance so that she could eventually become financially independent. She called the travelogue she wrote "The wanderings of a pariah".

This Latin American journey played a decisive role in the intellectual and political education of Flora Tristan. Through it she discovered misery, social oppression, class exploitation, sexual discrimination and social rebellions. It affected her so much that she decided to dedicate her life to the unification of the working class and women's emancipation. Although she managed to survive her husband's attempt to assassinate her with a pistol, she would not survive the exhaustion of the 1844 tour to promote *The Workers' Union* among laboring people. She was trying to win workers over to the need to build an international association. She died of fatigue and typhoid in the same year.

It is not by chance that women's liberation and social liberation came together in the life and works of Flora Tristan. There had already been decades of timid, tentative moves in this direction. Obviously there had been examples of women's resistance and attempts to win a margin of independence and freedom – joining heretical groups, religious involvement, the closed convent, mysticism, rudimentary medical practice and having specific social functions on the margin of the community. However these were individual efforts to escape oppression, which obviously took on diverse forms depending on a woman's class background.

The English and then the French revolutions created for the first time the conditions for thinking about women's liberation in collective terms. The pressure and control traditionally exerted over women were weakened by several processes: the subversion of a social order based on religion which was considered unchangeable until then, the shake-up of rigid social relations, and the raising of ideals of equality (even if framed in male terms). The bourgeois revolutions opened up cracks and created a new democratic space within which the idea began to emerge that if there was to be freedom and equality it could not exclude half the population.

In this way the English Diggers and Ranters already challenged the double standards of contemporary sexual morality where sexual freedom was the exclusive property of men. They also began to clearly trace the links between private property and sexual relations. Over a century later, on the other side of the Channel, Olympe de Gouges drew up the most comprehensive manifesto of bourgeois feminism during the French revolution: *The Declaration of the Rights of Women and Female Citizens.* She unmasked the so-called universalism of a revolution that up to then had been limited to thinking about the rights of *man* and *male citizens.* In her manifesto, Olympe de Gouges demanded full citizenship for women and for the right to take an active part in social and political life with legal, equal rights.

Two years later, Mary Wollstonecraft published *A Vindication of the Rights of Women.* In this book, based on a sharp analysis of the conditions of women, she showed how disparate conditions were not caused by nature but by education and she threw down a challenge to progressive and revolutionary men – if you want a better society you must also give women the education and instruction currently reserved only for yourselves. Fifty years later Mary Wollstonecraft aroused the enthusiasm of Flora Tristan. Wollstonecraft was another pariah – a truly hated figure for contemporary conservatives because of the scandalous way she conducted her private life and relationships. Nevertheless, between *Vindication* and the *Worker's Union* a real shift had taken place. Flora Tristan abandoned the tone of moral calls aimed mostly at men and synthesized, on one hand, her belief in the necessity of collective action involving women and, on the other, an understanding of the links between economic exploitation and women's oppression.

Some decades earlier in 1808, Charles Fourier, whom Flora Tristan knew personally, had published the *Theory of Four Movements* – a work that has had a profound impact on socialist feminist thinking. Fourier outlined the link between economic repression and women's sexual repression and made the condition of women a barometer for the level of social development. This theme was picked up also by Marx in the

1844 Economic and Philosophical Manuscripts. In Fourier's project of a cooperative community (which he developed in detail in subsequent works) women would finally have the right to the sexual freedom that was denied them in society through male power and the institution of the monogamous family. They would no longer be economically dependent on men. Looking after and educating children would become a community task, and women would be educated to the level needed to take an active role in social and political life.

In those years of ideological ferment, during the early days of the workers' movement, the utopian writings of people like William Thompson, Charles Fourier and Flora Tristan became the crucible where it was possible to bring together the ideals of social equality, the end of any exploitation and full women's emancipation. This was, however, a difficult and complex encounter which had to settle accounts with two correlated problems: on the one hand the lack of interest often shown by liberal feminists in the living conditions of women workers and their specific needs, and on the other hand, the suspicion and indifference shown by working-class women involved in social struggles to the demands raised by liberal feminists.

1.2 Ladies and working women

Parisian working women applauded the execution of Olympe de Gouges who was guillotined along with other Girondin leaders on 3 November 1793. Her call for woman's emancipation had not found support among women from the lower classes. This is not surprising. On the one hand Olympe de Gouges, just like the other representatives of bourgeois revolutionary feminism, never showed any particular interest in the living conditions of working women. On the other hand while the laws on divorce or measures in favour of greater equality between the sexes – for example in education – had aroused sympathy among working women, unemployment, misery and inflation were seen as much greater problems for them.

In any case, the French Revolution was certainly not the only event in which women had gone into the streets to protest, often in a radical way, and to demand bread. Since the responsibility for managing the family finances and looking after the children and ill or old family members fell historically on women's shoulders, it was often women who were the detonators of social revolts caused by misery and hunger. Linking up women's experiences in these episodic social and political struggles with an emerging feminism whose protagonists were women from the middle or upper classes was far from easy.

This feminism came to be known by the organizations of the workers' movement as bourgeois feminism. This definition, which was also challenged within the feminist movement, at times took on a negative or liquidationist connotation due to a certain conservatism with regard to the demands raised by these feminists. The emergent liberal or bourgeois feminist movement generally focused on two main axes. Firstly, the demand for access to education and culture which was, at times, linked to calls for women to have the right to a full professional career. Secondly, demands for civil and political rights, above all the right to own property and inherit it, but also divorce and the right to vote. Often these demands did not link up with demands for social justice, and bourgeois women showed a lack of understanding of the specific conditions and consequently the specific needs of working women. Notwithstanding a common oppression, its specific forms varied significantly according to social class.

Henrik Ibsen's play *The Doll's House*, written in 1879, portrayed the situation of Nora, a bourgeois woman, obliged to live the uselessness and emptiness of an inactive but cosseted life, to play the role of a mere ornament whose feminine qualities were essentially expressed in gracefulness, beauty and submissiveness. This life had little in common with that of a working woman who had to not just work for more than ten hours a day in the factory, but also manage the family home, making many sacrifices and undergoing repeated pregnancies. A working woman in most cases lived in a contradictory situation. She worked in the system of production, but doing so did not allow her to be economically independent from men. Women, in fact, were paid about half the rate for the same work and so, in the majority of cases, did not have the means to live on their own. In this situation only two paths were open: marriage or prostitution.

The blindness to this reality, the fact that bourgeois women's activism was often motivated by a demand for emancipation mainly on an individual level, made it difficult for the former to come together with the women who were beginning to organize, with many difficulties, inside the workers' movement. Often this was used as an excuse for the suspicious attitude of men from the workers' movement to feminist demands. It was the case, for example, with German bourgeois feminism, which was also characterized by a certain conservatism both on the questions of sexual freedom and civil rights. In 1865 the Allgemeine Deutsche Frauenverein (the General Association of German Women) was set up. This organization not only did not look for or establish any contacts with workers but limited itself to linking up with women from certain sectors of the petty bourgeoisie. It also did not include the extension of voting rights to women in its programme. Most of its demands only focused on access to education. It was only in 1902 that the bourgeois feminist movement included the demand for suffrage in its policies, but it did so without launching any real campaign. In terms of working regulations, it generally took a position against any regulations such as prohibiting women's night work, fearing that this type of legislation could lead to questioning women's right to work generally. In this way it showed a real blind spot concerning the unsustainable living conditions of working women, who, in addition to super-exploitation in the factory, had to take on a nurturing role at home which was made worse by lack of money, general misery and the absence of social services. All these factors, alongside some sectarianism from German social democratic women, made it very difficult and nearly impossible to build any unity of common interests around which women of different social classes could take action.

England was a different case. Here bourgeois feminism was to maintain a degree of dialogue with the workers' movement which, for its own part, was a little more open to the feminist struggle than elsewhere. Regardless of the reasons, the English trade-union movement's moderate views meant Marxist or revolutionary positions only had the support of a small minority, and the rise of socialist ideas was based more than anything else on moral condemnation of the alienation of human relations in capitalist society. Working-class women were therefore particularly subject to the influence of bourgeois feminists without being able to develop a radical, autonomous political line. The founding of the Women's Social and Political Union by Emmeline Pankhurst, supported by her daughter, Christabel Pankhurst, marked a new turning point in the relations between bourgeois feminism and working women. This movement, which was initially linked to the Independent Labour Party, became progressively transformed, under the influence of Christabel, into a pressure group campaigning for women's suffrage, and thereby increasingly lost any representation of working women's interests. Between the end of 1906 and the beginning of 1907 it brought out hundreds of thousands of women in demonstrations, culminating in the enormous demonstration of 21 June 1908. However its ties with the working class became weaker, replaced by a "classless" political line which excluded any social or economic demands and focused exclusively on the campaign for women's votes. Even Sylvia Pankhurst's attempts to link the feminist cause with the working class were firmly opposed by her mother and sister.

1.3 On both sides of the Channel

In England women took part in the trade-union movement from the very beginning, from the first decades of the 19th Century. They played an important role, even creating independent organizations with their own leaderships. Then they took part in the Chartist movement, developing the Associations of Chartist Women. Things changed, however, when the trade-union movement became more formally structured towards the middle of the century. Once these new structures took shape around a base of skilled workers, they tended to exclude unskilled workers. Since women generally occupied the lowest ranks in the hierarchy of production, they became marginalized or directly excluded from the trade unions.

This situation changed with the birth of the new trade-union movement in 1888-9 following a series of workers' strikes that raged in a number of factories across the country. The conditions now existed for the creation of new trade-union organizations which were now open to both unskilled workers and women. Within twenty years, from 1886 to 1906, the number of women trade union members went up from 37,000 to 167,000. By 1914 it had reached 357,956. Women did not just join the unions but also set up their own women-only trade-union organizations which brought together women who worked in non-unionized sectors or in sectors where unions did not allow women to join. This is why Mary Macarthur founded the National Federation of Women Workers in 1906 and from that year to 1914 it grew from 2,000 to 20,000 members.

On the other side of the Channel, the working women of Paris, who in 1789 had marched on Versailles, once again showed their determination and courage during those few months when the Paris Commune was "wiping the slate of the past clean" and throwing up the bases of a new society. On 18 March 1871 Parisian women placed themselves in front of the bayonets of soldiers sent by Thiers to take the National Guard's artillery. These were the same cannons that Parisians had paid for in small contributions to defend the capital from a Prussian invasion. They fraternized with the troops, spoke with the soldiers and asked them whether they really intended to open fire against their husbands, brothers and sons. In this way the women made a decisive contribution to derailing Thiers' plans. The soldiers in fact mutinied, joined with the masses, and arrested their own officers. Women thus played a pivotal role at the start of that Paris Spring, and in those two brief months of the Paris Commune before it was subsequently drowned in blood in the last week of May.

Just about a month after 18 March, on 11 April, a women's organization was created: it was called the Women's Union for the Defence of Paris and the Care of the Wounded. This organization was originally set up to carry out welfare tasks but very soon began to operate outside those limits. Women who were members of the First International played a leading role. Above all there was Elizabeth Dmitrieff, the daughter of a Russian noble who fled Russia to take refuge first in Switzerland and then in London where she made contact with Marx. The Union's April Manifesto was one of the most advanced documents produced during the Commune. It contained a miscellany of ideas and propositions, coming from different currents of nineteenth century socialism and French republicanism – such as the followers of Henri Saint Simon, Pierre-Joseph Proudhon or Louis Auguste Blanqui, radical republicanism, internationalism – which were at the heart and soul of the lively, often confused discussions of the *communards*. The *Manifesto* took a clear position in favour of social revolution, the overcoming of capitalism, and the end of any sort of exploitation. It also called on women to take an active role in the revolution.

The Union carried out welfare and support work for the Commune that women would normally undertake, particularly looking after the wounded during the fighting, but also distributing food and managing funds that were collectively raised. However, the Union rather quickly also took on an important role in the Labour Commission. The latter put forward a clear policy favouring the promotion of women's work and had projects to set up exclusively female workshops. It also launched the idea of a women's trade-union organization and asked for more opportunities for women to take an active part in the political and social life of the Commune. Out of the 128 members of the Union, the majority belonged to the working class and thus played a central role in production.

In pre-1870 Paris there were close to 550,000 highly skilled workers, mostly working in small and medium-sized manufacturing of an artisan nature. Large scale industry was a small part of overall production. Alongside these workers there were an enormous number of smaller, artisan workshops and poor intellectuals. Unlike in 1848, the years prior to the Franco-Prussian war, and even those during the war itself, saw a strong proletarianization of the petty-bourgeoisie and intellectual layers, which explains their changed attitude compared to 1848 when they joined forces with the National Guard to act as the armed wing of anti-working class repression. Women played a fundamental role in the productive system. Women's participation became even more important due to the economic crisis and mass unemployment resulting from the war. During the Commune, working-class employment fell from 550,000 to 114,000 – of whom more than half were women. The centrality of women's work in the politics of the Commune is therefore partially explained by its relative weight in the workforce during that period.

Notwithstanding the strict limits and the prejudice that continued to exist in the political actions of the Commune, some of the political and social measures taken clearly represented an improvement in women's living conditions. Among others, a special women-only commission was set up to work on the creation of female schools in order to give women access to education. A women-only technical school was established. Nurseries started to be set up near factories and workshops so that women's lives and working conditions could be improved. Finally, workshops employing only women were established and, on the suggestion of the internationalists, particularly Elizabeth Dmitrieff, a discussion was started on the topic of equal pay. A decree on 10 April awarded a pension to the widows and orphans of communards fallen in the cause, irrespective of the formal marital status of the women concerned. In this way a sort of equivalence was established between "common law" couples and those formally married, which in practice challenged traditional morality. Repression swiftly put an end to these embryonic measures and it is difficult to measure how they would have further evolved if that were not the case.

Alongside the Women's Union, other women's organizations emerged in various areas of Paris such as the women's local vigilance committees which initially organized welfare. Some women also took part in meetings of women-only vigilance committees. Among these was Louise Michel. A long-time secular and republican activist and a teacher, Louise Michel immediately supported the Commune, joining the Montmartre vigilance committee. She tirelessly worked on welfare tasks, was involved in the social and civil reforms, and fought in the front line of the women's battalion. She gave herself up to the Versailles regime after the fall of the Commune in order to free her mother who had been arrested in her place. Contrary to the expectations of her jailers, who had not wasted any time in ordering her deportation to New Caledonia, she used her trial to declare her passionate faith in the revolutionary cause:

"I do not want to defend myself and I do not wish to be defended, I totally support the social revolution and I am fully responsible for my actions ... You need to exclude me from society, you have been assigned that task. Good! The charge I face is the correct one. It seems that every heart that beats for freedom has only the right to a piece of lead, so let me have mine!"

This courage was not rare. During that bloody final week, women worked tirelessly to erect barricades where they fought in the front line defending Paris streets yard by yard from the advancing Versailles troops. A battalion of 120 women set up a barricade between Place Blanche and Boulevard Clichy which they defended heroically for a whole day despite many being killed. After the defeat of the Commune, 1,051 women were brought before the war tribunals, of whom 756 were working women, 246 were not in paid work, and only one was of bourgeois origin. The freedom and courage of the women communards were such that they provoked an out and out witchhunt in the press of the Versailles regime.. The legend of the *pétroleuses* (women using petroleum or paraffin to burn things down), of the Paris working woman of lax morals who roamed the city with incendiary intentions, was created precisely to stigmatize the glimpse of liberty offered by the Commune to women. Bourgeois and aristocratic women were the most relentless, particularly against their own sex. Prosper Lissagaray, one of the Commune's prominent activists who fled to England, where he became the partner of Eleanor Marx, tells the story of elegant women promenading in the streets of Paris in the weeks following the fall of the Commune when the continuous shootings of the communards became a pleasing spectacle for them. The French bourgeoisie watched approvingly as 30,000 communards were shot and 40,000 were deported in what was truly a class genocide. Among the fallen were the *pétroleuses*.

1.4 Social Democratic Parties

In Germany the history of the relations between the workers' movement and women's liberation is associated with two key figures: August Bebel and Clara Zetkin. In 1878 August Bebel published a book that was to go down in history, *Women under Socialism*, in which he denounced the unsustainable situation of the working woman and her dual oppression (as a worker and as a woman). Arguing against the position of Lassalle, who held an opposite view, Bebel saw women joining the workforce as a determinant precondition of their emancipation. The book had a formidable impact in the internal discussions of German social democracy and along with *The Origins of the Family, Private Property and the State*, published by Friedrich Engels six years later, remained for a long time the key reference point for Marxist feminism.

Bebel's position for full participation of women in the workforce as a precondition for their emancipation was adopted as the political position for the German Social Democratic Party (SDAP) founded at the Eisenach Congress in 1869. In 1875, when this party merged with Ferdinand Lassalle's party to form the German Socialist Workers Party (SAPD), the

Lassallians' proposal to ban women from working in industry was defeated at the founding congress. Twenty years later, in 1895, women still only made up 11.8 per cent of the working class in manufacturing and industry, increasing only to 12.9 per cent by 1907 (1,540,000).

While one may be tempted to see Clara Zetkin's theoretical contribution as less salutary, the birth of the socialist feminist movement in Germany cannot be understood without properly situating her political and organizational contributions. Clara Zetkin worked tirelessly for years organizing women inside German social democracy. Thanks to her pressure, the Second International's 1889 Congress agreed a resolution in favour of women working in industry and for equal pay for equal work. A decision was taken in 1890 to establish a publication that would advocate for working women. It was edited by Clara Zetkin and came out in 1891 with the name *Die Arbeiterin* or *Working Woman* and then changed its name in 1892 to *Die Gleichheit* or *Equality*. The political programme defended by the newspaper included the extension of both passive and active voting rights to women; the end of laws discriminating against women, above all freeing women to meet and participate in political activity; free education; the suspension of night work, the reduction of the working day to eight hours and the banning of child labour. From a theoretical point of view, Zetkin's newspaper took as its reference the positions developed by Bebel and Engels. In the years leading up to the First World War *Equality* was the last party publication to remain in the hands of the left, revolutionary wing which strongly opposed the First World War. Its circulation rose from a few thousand copies in the early years to 23,000 copies in 1905 and then up to 112,000 in 1913.

Demands raised in this period focused particularly on women's work, education and its role, and the necessity of sharing domestic labour inside the family. The family as such, however, was hardly ever at the centre of the debate, nor was the question of sexuality and birth control. Contrary to what was to happen during the Russian revolution, above all thanks to

Alexandra Kollontai's writings, the question of free love was not particularly discussed. Demands remained rather centred on the class organization of women and their right to vote whereas policies on sexual matters tended to be more moralistic.

Notwithstanding these limits, the German Social Democratic party certainly supported the most progressive positions within a German context where bourgeois feminists had much more moderate positions, not only in terms of challenging traditional sexual roles, but even on the level of political and civil rights. For many years the Social Democrats were the only political organization to not only include but campaign on a programme that included women's right to vote. At the same time it was the only party where women could find the space and means for self-organizing and expressing their needs. The forms of independent organization within the party were initially created to get around laws which prevented women from going to political meetings. So these forms of organization were not based on a reflection on the necessity for and value of women-only meetings, but rather on the need to respond to a specific difficulty of discriminatory laws against women. In 1908, however, after the latter laws had been repealed, the rights of women to continue to have separate meetings, to elect their own leadership, and to have their own publication, were maintained. In fact some years before a national commission for women's campaigns and action had been elected by women themselves. Thanks to this experience, initially dictated by external constraints, Clara Zetkin and others understood how useful women-only discussion and organization could be for both giving women confidence and encouraging them to become more politically active.

Up to 1900 there were scarcely any women organized in the Social Democratic party or the trade unions. In 1891 there were only 4,355 women trade unionists (1.8 per cent of trade-union members), by 1900 there were 22,844 (3.3. per cent). There were 4,000 women in the party in 1905, 29,458 in 1908, 82,642 in 1910 and 141,115 by 1913. The significant growth in female membership, however, must be situated relative to the overall growth of the party. In any case, before the First World War women never comprised more than 10 per cent of party membership.

The indefatigable activity of Clara Zetkin and other social democrats committed to organizing women party members and workers was decisive on an international scale. In 1907 the first International Conference of Socialist Women took place with the participation of 60 delegates coming from 16 countries. Also in 1907, the Seventh Congress of the Socialist International was held and there was a big debate on women's right to vote. At the time an argument was very prevalent that women were more influenced by religious and reactionary forces than men, and therefore their votes would favour right wing and conservative political parties. Nevertheless, a resolution was adopted to support a campaign for the extension of women's voting rights. These conferences certainly represented a step forward in the debate within the Socialist International, but at the same time, because of the non-binding nature of such resolutions on individual parties, the policies were a dead letter in a good number of countries.

The second Conference of Socialist Women took place, in tandem with the Eighth Congress of the Socialist International in Copenhagen in 1910, with one hundred delegates (men and women), coming from 17 countries. It was on this occasion that International Women's Day was instituted, initially without a fixed date. The 8 March date was established later, after women lit the touch paper of the Russian Revolution when they demonstrated on the streets of Petrograd on 23 February 1917 – the equivalent of 8 March in all other countries.

1.5. Revolutionary women.

The Petrograd women demonstrated spontaneously and in defiance of the orders of their existing organizations on 23 February, 1917 (8 March) to celebrate International Women's Day, after having also convinced their male co-workers to support the strike. They certainly did not imagine what momentous events their action would trigger. Hunger, unbearable working conditions, and the crisis caused by the war – all these factors impelled them into the streets to demand bread and peace. Instead of a demonstration about immediate demands it became the start of the Russian revolution.

Despite the limits, the backward steps, the conservative reaction, and the serious difficulties arising from the Civil War and the collapse of the economy, the first years of the Russian revolution certainly represented the highpoint of the process of women's emancipation. In no other historical event had women been able to benefit from such freedom and dignity, enjoy full citizenship rights, actively participate in political and social life, dynamically contribute to building a new social and political order, and simply be in charge of their own lives. Before the revolution the various theorists of the Bolshevik party had already placed great importance on women's liberation. Years of exile, living underground, deportations and systematic exclusion from ordinary social life meant that many of them were contemptuous of conventional norms and traditional – particularly petty-bourgeois – family relations. Life on the margins, always on the move, and solidarity among exiled comrades had in part liberated them from the conservative morality that characterized workers' movements in other countries. The family was seen, for the most part, as a place where oppression was perpetuated and conservative, reactionary values, prejudices and superstitions were inculcated. It was seen as an obstacle to a fuller, richer social life outside the walls of domesticity. Revolutionaries counterposed a positive alternative framework where people would seek more authentic relations based on reciprocal respect and not on hierarchical and dependent economic interests.

The axes of women's liberation, according to the proposals and writings of the Bolsheviks, were based on two central elements: the freeing up of women from domestic labour, and independence from men through full participation in the workforce. Freedom from domestic labour was to come from its progressive socialization, in other words, through collective arrangements for child or adult care which would stop being a private matter carried out within the family household. It was a case of setting up a series of services – nurseries, laundries and canteens – which would have progressively achieved that objective. Solving the problem of the double exploitation of women, therefore, became identified with the socialization of domestic labour rather than through challenging traditional roles inside the family and the sexual division of labour. In fact it was considered quite natural for women to carry out the caring work in nurseries, laundries and canteens – but as salaried workers rather than mothers or wives. Women were considered more pre-disposed to this sort of work. However, the objective of freeing up time for women, allowing them to actively take part in political and social life, and opening them up to more revolutionary ideas, was clearly maintained.

Following the political line of Engels, Bebel and Clara Zetkin, the Bolsheviks also placed great importance on the full integration of women into the workforce. In order to be really free, women had to be economically independent of men. Monogamous and heterosexual relations were not put up for debate as such, and positions on homosexuality were more backward. It was hoped that there would be a radical transformation through the weakening of family ties and of interpersonal relations based on economic dependency. As for monogamy, it was not challenged as such but inside the Bolshevik party one could see the development of a discussion on free love, or rather on the nature of affection and sexual relationships. This was practically absent from the debates inside German social democracy.

Alexandra Kollontai played a key role in these discussions. Not only did she emphasize these questions in her writings, but also struggled for years against the conservatism of many party members and leaders. She belonged to the Menshevik current in exile but joined the Bolshevik party in 1915. After much persistence she managed, in 1917, to get the party to set up a department in charge of working with women. In 1919 it was transformed into Zhenotdel – the Women's Section of the Central Committee of the Russian Communist Party. Within the party Kollontai found Vladimir Lenin a very significant supporter. The latter, thanks to the close collaboration and ongoing exchange of views with his wife, Nadezhda Krupskaya, and with Ines Armand, had fully understood the need for there to be a specific intervention around the particular problems facing women. Without policies able to respond to the problems and needs of women it would indeed not be possible to free them from conditions of economic dependency and of double exploitation, which was the basis of their conservative political tendencies. If you wanted to win women – the most backward element of Russian society – to the revolutionary cause, it was necessary to develop a political line that responded to their specific oppression. Alongside Lenin, there were other Bolshevik leaders who showed themselves particularly open and understood the need to encourage a greater female presence and participation in both the party and the soviets. Among these we can single out Leon Trotsky and Yakov Sverdlov who, up to his death in 1919, gave Kollantai great organizational support.

To fully understand the scale of the measures and reforms made after the October revolution one must refer back to the conditions of women in Tsarist society. Tsarist laws obliged women to obey their husbands as the head of the family, submit to his will in all circumstances, and follow him wherever he went. Women could not take a job or get a passport without the authorization of the head of the family. Divorce was very difficult because it was ultimately authorized by the Orthodox Church and, in any case, its cost placed it outside the reach of the poor. To make matters worse, domestic violence was prevalent. In peasant families it was customary for the father of the bride to present his son-in-law with a whip, to be used in case of need. In the countryside women had the added burden of working in the fields alongside husbands, fathers and brothers in addition to the domestic labour of washing, spinning, weaving, cooking, carrying water, taking care of children, old people and the ill... In the towns they worked the same hours as the men but were paid a lot less without benefiting from any protective labour laws. For some of those suffering from hunger, occasional prostitution became the ultimate recourse. Pregnancy could cause dramatic problems and, at times, pushed women to infanticide.

So the condition of a woman in Tsarist Russia was akin to that of a slave. The revolution made her a citizen.

In the period immediately after the October Revolution a series of measures were implemented aiming at the heart of the traditional family and the patriarchal authority. The newly-instituted Family Code of 1918 allowed easy access to divorce; abolished the obligation for women to take their husband's surname; abolished the attribution of "head of family" to the man and therefore established equal rights for both partners; eliminated the distinction between legitimate and illegitimate children; and abrogated the obligation to follow the husband if he moved to another area. The power of the Church was abolished and the interference of the state in marital relations was kept to a minimum. The Family Code was updated in 1927 and made access to divorce even simpler, legally recognized cohabiting couples, and laid down an obligation for divorced couples to pay for food for at least 12 months to a partner who was unemployed or unable to work. In 1920 a decree legalized abortion. The Soviet Union, therefore, became the first state in the world to give women the right to legal, free abortions. The December 1917 law on national sickness insurance was the start of a series of measures setting up social security for women's work. The right to 16 weeks maternity leave before and after birth was passed into law, as well as the right for pregnant women to do lighter work and to be excluded from being transferred to another job without the agreement of the work inspector.

A number of factors made the overall feminist project much more difficult than could have been foreseen: the terrible conditions resulting from the aftermath of the Civil War; the fierce resistance from peasants to the most progressive measures – including the attempts to set up nurseries in country villages

– and a growing lack of confidence among women workers themselves. Even though the Bolshevik government had sought to create a network of services that would have led to the progressive socialization of domestic labour, the collapse of the Soviet economy meant forward momentum in this area was severely held back. The number of nurseries were far from sufficient and the canteens served absolutely awful food. Furthermore, one of the first effects of the economic crisis was a new wave of women's unemployment. As a consequence, most women remained economically dependent on men and continued to be responsible for domestic labour. In these circumstances prostitution born of misery was widespread.

The serious deterioration in economic conditions and the consequent slowdown in the implementation of policies favouring women certainly contributed to their growing passivity and mistrust in a revolutionary government that had promised to radically change their situation. Notwithstanding the great efforts of Zhenotdel, Alexandra Kollontai and other leaders and activists, there were only 30,000 women in the party in 1923 – mostly of working-class origin.

While the policies put forward by the government of the soviets were broadly supported by urban women, the relationship with peasant women was much more problematic – in 1923 the latter made up only five per cent of women party members. In most cases the proposed policies were treated with great suspicion, even the village nurseries seemed to confirm a myth according to which the new government wanted to take babies away from their families. Obviously the backwardness of the countryside, superstitious beliefs, prejudice, and the strength of patriarchal structures explain to a large extent the peasant women's hostile reaction. There is, however, a stronger explanation to be found in the particular circumstances peasant women found themselves in during the Civil War. Alongside the serious economic situation that made it hard to implement policies, one must remember how weak the soviets were in the countryside. They were not able to protect women from male violence and harassment. The Great War and then the Civil War had resulted in a very high number of both widows and women without husbands, many of whom tried to cultivate their pieces of land without any help from men.

These women were subject to a real process of expropriation by men who, arguing that women's labour was not sufficiently productive, were able to get land redistributed in their favour. It left women with the smallest, least fertile parcels of land. Women peasants who tried to assert their rights often became subject to denigration and scorn and, in most cases, the soviets were not able to put a stop to these situations. Moreover, there were cases of violence, and even murder, against many of those who decided to take part in women's meetings organized by the soviets or the local sections of the Bolshevik party. In these conditions the majority of peasant women clung to the old patriarchal structures, that is, to matrimony and the family, however much these were the source of their specific oppression. It still seemed safer to hang on to traditional structures when faced with the dual uncertainties of social castigation and the need to feed oneself and one's family.

Revolutionary Russia was, at least up to the end of the 1920s, the place where women were able to taste unprecedented freedom. This was despite the enormous objective difficulties, the limits of the actions of the Bolsheviks and their contradictions, and the lack of reflection about women's sexual self-determination and gender identity. In no other historical event have we seen so clearly the links between women's emancipation, self-organization and the workers' movement. After Stalinism had established its grip and infected the politics of the communist parties organized in a now bureaucratized Third International, those links were utterly destroyed.

1.6 Women fighters

A few years before the Spanish Civil War, nobody could have imagined the sight of courageous and determined women fighting in the front ranks against the Falangists who had come to drown their dream of a better, fairer society in blood. Spanish women had, in fact, always been excluded from politics and social life, kept uneducated and subject to the omnipresent influence of a particularly reactionary Catholic Church. They became politicized very late. A few months of Civil War was enough for them to catch up. In the Spain of 1931 women made up only 12 per cent of the workforce but were present in great numbers in some of the most militant industrial sectors and factories – particularly the textile workers who played a key role in Catalonia. In 1913, 22,000 of the 26,300 workers involved in the textile workers' strike in Barcelona were women. In 1936 nearly a fifth of textile workers were in Catalonia and women comprised a large majority of the workforce in this industry. They worked eleven hours a day and on average were paid half the male salary. The worst working conditions were, however, those of the farm workers who were forced to work up to eighteen hours a day without a break and who often received only salary in kind. A quarter of the female workforce worked in this sector. Women were further disadvantaged by their gross illiteracy rates: in 1931 ninety per cent of the women in the countryside and eighty per cent in the towns were illiterate.

The 1931 constitution adopted by the Republican government was certainly in advance of the political consciousness of Spanish women. It established women's right to vote, be elected, and formal gender equality. Related laws also banned employment contracts which permitted the sacking of women if they got married, sought more equal pay, and established mixed schooling. Other measures followed these laws. In 1932 a divorce law was passed which recognized the right to divorce through mutual consent with custody of children going to the wife. "Honour" crimes were also banned in that year. In 1933 a law was passed against prostitution. Finally, in 1936 an abortion law was adopted. These laws, which were all removed after Franco's victory, were promulgated in the absence of a significant women's movement, even a bourgeois feminist one.

The minor role of women in the workforce, combined with the great influence of the Catholic Church and a culture that accepted a certain "machismo" created a situation where women were forced to be largely passive recipients of their political fortune. Women only began to mobilize in the months immediately prior to the Civil War. Initially, the disorganization of the regular army meant that women could actively participate in the fighting and take important roles in the struggle. They showed incredible courage. The Anarchists were the first to call women to arms.

Between 1936 and 1938 around sixty to seventy per cent of women took a job outside the home to replace men engaged at the front. Despite the decision of Caballero, the war minister, to exclude them from the regular army, the Civil War opened up enormous opportunities for women to become active and organize. They finally became more fully integrated in the workforce, they took part in mass organizations. They could at last get directly involved in political and social life. The specific conditions of being at war also contributed to the mass entry of women into the workforce in other countries. Here it was combined with the cauldron of political activity and the emergence of women's publications. There was an accelerated growth in their politicization.

One of the most advanced examples of women's politicization was *Mujeres Libre* (Free Women) which came out of an initiative taken by a group of women from the Madrid trade-union federation. In 1935 they were convinced of the need for a women-only organization. The group published a magazine and set up literacy classes and seminars. By 1938 it had become a league of 30,000 women, mostly working-class, with about 150 groups throughout Spain. Although not comprising only anarchists, the group considered itself to be part of the anarchist movement. In its August 1937 Congress it set up a federal structure based on the autonomy of local groups, a coordinating committee, and six secretariats. The fact that it was set up before the Civil War meant this group had much longer-term political perspectives. It was founded with the understanding that women needed to struggle independently in order to build their own consciousness and to further their struggle for emancipation.

Consequently it launched two literacy campaigns, organized courses and created institutes with libraries in Valencia, Madrid and Barcelona. Women's right to employment was one of its key demands.

Faced with the conservatism of other Spanish workers' organizations, *Mujeres Libres* argued against the idea that women's employment was merely a substitution in times of war. It campaigned to set up nurseries in the workplace whether in factories, rural areas, or the public sector. This group also criticized the anarchist campaign for sexual freedom that had led many men to behave in a way that was against women's interests. The question these women raised was "Okay, sexual freedom, but for whom?" This question was to be at the centre of debates during the second wave of feminism, in the second half of the twentieth century. In Spain, however, the discussions about self-determination with respect to maternity, control of their own bodies, and prostitution continued to be riddled with many contradictions.

1.7. Women in the Chinese revolution.

The oppressive conditions suffered by women in pre-revolutionary China are unparalleled. Middle-class women could hardly own any property except their jewellery, and were not allowed to inherit anything. Their feet were bandaged and they were excluded from practically all productive employment. They were relegated to the role of a household ornament, totally dependent on and subject to a husband's authority. Furthermore, a second marriage in the case of widowhood was very much frowned on. Without land or means of sustenance, single women could not have an independent life in Chinese society. Peasant women had slighly more autonomy due to their role as agricultural labourers. This was, however, a very relative autonomy which was paid for dearly through incessant work, misery, and domestic violence.

By the nineteenth century some voices had already spoken out against this situation. Li Ju-chen wrote a utopian romantic novel in 1825 where he described a kingdom governed by women in which men were completely subservient – a scenario that overturned then existing gender relations. A growing number of women, supported by Christian organizations (particularly Protestants), began to oppose arranged marriages. Finally, various women began to join organizations opposed to the political regime and to colonialism – such as the secret societies that played a role in the 1911 revolution.

Despite these early gains, the decisive moment in advancing the struggle was made when the growing workers' movement combined with the movement opposed to Japanese imperialism. During the First World War radical groups open to women were formed in which women's situation in the family and the need for a reform of marriage laws were discussed. In 1919 Mao Zedong had already published a series of articles on women's oppression where he supported the extension of voting rights to women and other forms of equality. The newspaper, *Women's Voice*, was founded in 1921, at the same time as the Chinese Communist Party, and it proclaimed the necessity of improving women's working conditions. After the 1927 split between the Communist Party and the Nationalists, and the turn of the latter towards Confucianism and a strongly anti-feminist ideology, the communists continued to put forward a policy clearly in favour of women's liberation. They began to raise these issues even in the rural areas where they were forced to retreat following the Nationalists' victory and the subsequent anti-communist persecution.

Following the Second World War and the victory in the Civil War against the Nationalists, the Communist victory inaugurated a period of major reforms that aimed at radically changing women's roles and living conditions. During the Civil War numerous women's organizations had emerged in the liberated zones. Ten months before the proclamation of the People's Republic, the Preparatory Committee for the All-China Women's Federation called a national congress in order to rationalize and unify the working women's organizations that were operating in various parts of the country. The idea was to bring together these associations so they could establish local sections of the national Women's Federation.

Article 6 of the September 1949 Constitution declared: "The Chinese People's Republic abolishes the feudal system which kept women in slavery. Women will have the same rights as men in politics, the economy, culture, education and social life. Freedom of marriage is guaranteed in law for men and women." A series of measures was subsequently implemented to give substance to this declaration, above all in favour of women's economic independence. The May 1950 Land Reform law finally gave women access to land ownership. Alongside this, the new marriage laws ended the practice of forced marriages and guaranteed equal rights for men and women within the family and the right to monogamy. This defence of monogamy may raise a few eyebrows today given the debate on sexual freedom, but it had quite a different meaning in 1940s China where the concubine system and bigamy were important elements of women's oppression. Other laws adopted included: the right to divorce on mutual consent; the right to take an active part in society; the right to independently administer one's own finances; and the right to freely choose one's career.

In 1951 the social security and welfare law was passed, which guaranteed 56 days of paid maternity leave before and after the birth date. It also banned the firing of pregnant women and provided sickness benefits for men and women. More than elsewhere, women could find space for autonomy and independence in agricultural communes. Every woman rural worker received a personal salary based on work done, and the communes had the added benefit establishing communal canteens, nurseries, and old people's hospices. This freed women from a large part of their domestic labour and gave them the time to actively participate in politics and social life. The proliferation of women's associations and organizations also in the countryside showed an enthusiastic involvement that was completely new in Chinese society. Throughout the 1950s various campaigns promoted contraception with positive meetings, film showings, expositions, and conferences. Abortion was theoretically legal but this did not mean that rural women had easy access to it.

Obviously the Chinese revolution also came up against the same difficulties as the Russian revolution in its attempts to change gender relations. While agrarian reform had been immediately welcomed by women peasants, since they could see its demonstrable advantage in making an independent life increasingly possible, challenging traditional family structures ran into greater resistance in the countryside. Furthermore, the Chinese women's movement held onto a certain puritanism for a long time, not so much because of any moralistic attitudes but because for centuries women had paid in flesh and blood for male sexual freedom.

1.8. The new feminism

During the first wave of feminism, the demand for emancipation had allowed links to be made between bourgeois feminism and feminists inside the workers' movement, and even led to unity of action in certain circumstances. Demands for access to education and employment, for full citizenship and the right to take part in politics were key, shared concerns. The first wave of feminism campaigned for the inclusion of all those who had always been excluded and fought for the full achievement of the equal rights promised by the French Revolution. Demanding equality with men was not necessarily subordination to the male framework – a criticism often made against this first wave. It was rather that the conceptual tools which the bourgeois revolutions and then the workers' movement had made available were taken up by women in order to bring out their most radical dynamic. "Equality cannot be real unless it is made with us" was the challenge thrown down by feminists to those who, under the cover of a false universalism, had conceived these values up to now only in male terms.

The second wave of feminism which rose up between the middle of the 1960s and the 1970s radically questioned this paradigm. In the period between the two waves of feminism, in 1949, a book had been published that was to become groundbreaking – it was Simone de Beauvoir's *The Second Sex.*

The new feminism developed out of a whole range of the 1960s and 1970s movements – students and youth, new workers' rebellions, national liberation struggles, civil rights and black power. With these movements that spread throughout the planet, feminism found the lifeblood for its resurgence in the huge blows struck against the existing social and political order by a new generation of "the ungrateful children of prosperity"; by the politicized students in the campuses of Europe and the USA, by the new black movement in the USA, and by a young rebellious working class. While it is true that the second wave of feminism was also a time of divorce between feminism and the workers' movement, the extension, strength and radicalism of women's struggles and the theoretical developments associated with them are unimaginable without the favourable context created by 1968 and the movements that followed. Youth rebellions challenged existing society, criticizing not only the relations of production but also social relations. They challenged the stereotypes and frameworks imposed on them, the culture of conformity and the conservativism behind the often voiced idea that "you've never have had it so good". They took on authoritarianism and a myriad of social power relations. The new feminists found critical instruments to use against the sexist domination of culture, society, production, politics, and the family within this radical challenge to existing society and among the attempts to try out different social and sexual relationships.

One of the characteristic features of the second feminist wave was the replacement of the emancipatory framework based on demanding equality with men with a refusal, in the name of a theory of difference(s), of an equality understood as subjection to a sexist, male framework. Demanding the right to difference was a powerful conceptual tool which was to bring about a split from the mixed social movements within which most of the feminists in the second wave had first become politicized. It was no longer enough to ask for full participation of women in politics and society. While the experience of activists from related struggles that had criticized politics and society was useful, this had not led to a real questioning of gendered power relations. Consequently, women began to systematically deconstruct and criticize the forms of politics, society and culture in order to expose their patriarchal nature. For thousands of years only men had access to the symbolic order, they had moulded it in their image so women were inevitably excluded from it. Not even the organization and political practices of the workers' movement were spared. In fact the workers' movement also echoed this exclusion of sexuality and gender relations from political discourse. Feminists felt this and denounced it as foreign to their own experience of politicization and intervention. A second common feature of this wave of feminism was the centrality of women's self-determination: the demand for free abortion and contraception on demand, along with the condemnation of male violence and new thinking about sexuality, which included radical theories on the violence and domination inherent in sexual intercourse.

Two more central features were:

1) Theorizing patriarchy as a system of oppression that pre-existed capitalism, and considering gender power relations as the matrix for all other forms of domination, oppression and exploitation. In short, there was a general rejection of accepting a hierarchy of contradictions which saw class at the top below which lay gender, race, nationality, etc;

2) Putting forward an idea of politics that draws the personal and the political together, and thereby theorizing an immediate transformation of self and of the forms of personal existence and relationships with other men and women.

In spite of the central importance given to new thinking about sexuality and its forms, the fundamental contribution made by lesbians to the feminist movement, as well as their frontline activism and visibility, did not always find favour. In countries like Italy this led to a growing friction between lesbians and the feminist movement, and ultimately to a split and the formation of a separate lesbian movement. The latter has sought to interpret lesbianism not simply as something pertinent to the field of sexuality, but as an eminently political position – the politics of those who are so far on the margins of an existing heterosexual order that they alone are able to carry out the most radical critique.

The origins of second wave feminism were rooted in the American college and university campuses of the 1960s. One of the major sources of inspiration for the movement were the African-American movements developing in that period that came to play a key role in the US protests of the 1960s. Feminism took some new conceptual tools from these movements: the discovery of difference as a process of affirmation and definition of one's identity; self-determination; and liberation struggle. As in other countries, second wave feminism was a movement made up mainly of young women, who had taken part in other movements – for free speech, for civil rights, and building the New Left. Women became conscious within these movements of the necessity of a separate women's movement in which there would be space for their specific needs and aspirations. Despite the massive involvement and fundamental role women played in these movements and organizations, they did not gain a corresponding leadership role as they were suffocated by sexist male leadership and methods of functioning. This tension became so blatant that it pushed women activists to bring their own gender-difference based demands to the fore.

Three books were published in 1970 that profoundly influenced not only the feminist movement in the United States, but also in many other countries: *The Dialectic of Sex* by Shulamith Firestone, *Sexual Politics* by Kate Millet and *Sisterhood is Powerful* by Robin Morgan. In the latter, Morgan, using the concept of sisterhood, puts forward the idea of a universal unity between all women against their common oppression, sexism. According to the author, sexism represents the matrix of all other oppression whether capitalist, racist or imperialist. This idea of universal sisterhood was strongly challenged by African-American, Chicana and working-class activists who refused to identify themselves within a hierarchy of oppression outlined by white radical feminists or as a part of a sisterhood that they accused of essentialism. While acknowledging the sexism that existed within their own mixed movements, these women activists could not identify with the "feminist category" defined by white feminists, nor give up their common struggle alongside the men in their community or class against their exploitation as workers and their oppression as African-Americans, immigrants or Chicanos. The black feminist Frances Beal, one of the founders of the Third World Women's Alliance, wrote a document entitled *Double Jeopardy* where she did not mince words: "It is useless to delude yourself into thinking about a black women's existence if you limit yourself to seeing her as looking after her house and children like a white middle-class woman. Most black women have to work to survive, to put food on the table and dress their families." As long as black women experience a double or triple oppression as women, as black people, and as workers, it is not possible to establish a hierarchy between the different struggles, putting one in front and relegating the others to secondary concerns.

United States feminism and Black Power were to deeply influence the British movement too, which more than many others maintained a rich dialogue with the workers' movement. This was partly due to the fact that the Communist Party was so weak it was not able to exert a significant influence as was the case in countries like France and Italy. So in Great Britain the first women's liberation groups emerging at the end of the 1960s kept up good links both with the student and workers' movements. They took part in debates about workers' control and supported workers' trade-union struggles. Feminists there theorized the links between home and work, production and reproduction, domestic and paid labour. They sought to create a movement together with workers and users of public services to radically reform the welfare state, to challenge gender roles inside the family, and the sexual division of labour outside it.

The first feminist group in Italy, the *Demau* (Demystification of Patriarchal Authoritarianism), was founded in 1965 and published its Programmatic Manifesto in 1966. A few years later, following the Italian youth rebellion, the foundations were laid for a new feminist movement. In 1969 the student movement linked up with the strongly rising new workers' movement which was very radical and very young. The tide of rebellion swelled throughout the next decade up to the momentous events of 1977. The new Italian feminists, for the most part – as elsewhere – were made up of young women who came out of the 1968 movement and often belonged to the New Left organizations that emerged in its wake. In 1970, the *Rivolta Femminile* (Feminine Revolt) and Anabasi groups were started, and Carla Lonzi wrote *Sputiamo su Hegel* (We Spit on Hegel), the founding text of Italy's new feminism. The real apex of the movement was reached in the period between 1974 and 1977. The first national meeting of feminist groups, which had sprung up all over Italy, was held in 1973 in the southern city of Pinarella. In 1970 a divorce law was finally put on the books. In 1974 the Italian people were asked in a referendum if they wanted to repeal this law, but over 59 per cent voted against repeal. The abortion campaign launched in 1975 ended in victory in 1978 with the passing of a law which, despite its serious limitations, introduced the right to free and legal abortions for the first time.

Italian feminism was also influenced by the United States radical feminists, and found a continuous source of inspiration in psychoanalysis and "French Theory". The feminist movement was impelled in this direction partly due to the hostility of the Italian Communist Party and the New Left organizations to autonomous women's organizations. It mostly took a separatist path, but at the same time there was an unprecedented wave of women's mobilizations inside the trade unions. Women's trade unionization was due in part to the rise in the number of women in the workforce – between 1973 and 1981 women provided 1,247,00 new workers while only 253,000 were men.

Other reasons for increasing unionization were the influence of other favorable social movements and the generally pro-worker political climate. The first groups of women trade unionists were set up in 1975, and their development was particularly strong in the big industrial centres where the working class was politically more active.

Just as in Italy, 1968 in France was characterized by the silence of women who had not been able to express themselves or play a leading role inside the movement. The Italian expression "angelo del ciclostile" – the angel of the duplicating machine – points to this exclusion. This was a recycling of the traditional "angel of the hearth" expression, in other words, from pots and pans to physically printing the leaflets indicates how the sexual division of labour had not changed. The French feminist movement of the early 1960s was similar to those in the United States and Italy. It was mostly made up of young women who were involved in the student movement and in the revolutionary left.

On 26 August 1970 some women placed flowers on the tomb of the Unknown Soldier in Paris stating: "There is someone even more unknown than the Unknown Soldier and that is his wife!" This symbolic act threw the spotlight of the mass media for the first time on the Mouvement de libération des femmes (MLF, women's liberation movement), a women-only organization, one of whose leaders was Monique Wittig. On 5 April 1971, 343 women published a manifesto in the magazine *Nouvel Observateur* declaring, to great consternation in French society, that they had had abortions. It was the starting point of the campaign for abortion rights which led to legislation in 1974. In the meantime, feminist groups and collectives were set up throughout France, in the neighbourhoods, in workplaces, and in the universities. They brought together demands for the freedom to control their own bodies with a criticism of patriarchy and sexism inside the mixed organizations of the workers' movement and the New Left.

Chapter 2
... AND DIVORCES

2.1 A problem from the start

It would be quite wrong to think that the coming together of feminism and the workers' movement would happen naturally, without contradictions or difficulties. In the first place, as we have already shown, feminism originally emerged within the corner of liberty opened up by the bourgeois revolution and was first theorized by middle-class and upper-middle-class women. In the second place every workers' movement is a child of its time. It is unhistorical to think that its members, leaders and theoreticians would be naturally free of prejudice, stereotypical attitudes and resistance to feminism. Their reaction is the fruit of thousands of years of women's oppression. Finally alongside this long term historical context, we can add other subsequent reasons resulting from specific historical processes such as the bureaucratic degeneration of the Soviet Union and its impact within the international workers' movement, and the internal dynamics of the New Left groups formed in the 1960s and 1970s.

Whatever our judgment on his relations with women in his private life, the young Marx did write in the 1844 *Economic and Philosophical Manuscripts*:

"In the relationship with woman, as the spoil and handmaid of communal lust, is expressed the infinite degradation in which man exists for himself."

Engels and Bebel wrote two books which for a long time were the primary references for socialist feminism; in these the relationship between men and women was compared to that between a capitalist and the proletarian. Fourier saw the female condition as a barometer of how civilized a society is and proposed a radical shake up of sexual roles... However Pierre-Joseph Proudhon, one of the leaders of the developing nineteenth-century workers' movement, was a complete misogynist.

Proudhon was a strenuous defender of the family and of a woman's role as determined by nature. He was firmly against women going to work outside the family home. Even worse he declared women should naturally submit to men as their subordinates. Contrary to their claims for equality, women were naturally inferior to men morally, physically and intellectually. He unreservedly condemned any project of women's liberation pursued by women themselves, and obviously there was no question of broaching the issue of sexual freedom.

This political stance was not exceptional and it is not surprising that the First International did not envisage the participation of women. We can see how misogynist prejudice played out dramatically in the story of Jeanne Deroin. She was an editorial board member of *Voix des Femmes* (Women's Voice), a founder of another newspaper, *L'Opinion des femmes* (Women's Opinion), she was heavily involved in the feminist movement and actively supported workers in the 1848 French Revolution. Between August 1849 and May 1850, Deroin dedicated herself to building an association of workers' organizations based on parity of rights for women and men. She also wrote the programmatic documents for this association. In May 1850, 400 workers' organizations emerging in the wake of the 1848 revolution joined the association. When Jeanne Deroin was arrested on 29 May 1850 and accused of conspiracy, her comrades asked her not to reveal her role in the organization. If it were to be known that a woman had built it up and written its programme, the workers' association would be generally discredited. Torn between her strong feminist convictions and the desire not to damage the workers' organizations, Jeanne

Deroin capitulated in the end and decided not to unveil her secret. Exile in England following Napoleon III's coup d'etat marked the erasing of her name from our history. Jeanne Deroin had to wait for the second feminist wave for her place in history to be restored.

Ferdinand Lassalle in Germany also took a position against women working outside the home, in defence of the traditional family. He represented a rather common political line within the workers' movement. From the start, when women's labour was generally paid much less than men's and the rate of female employment was very much lower, women were seen as a threat for male workers insofar as they were an enormous, low paid reserve army of labour. Lassalle did not think one should fight the competition of low paid women's labour by demanding equal pay and rights of all workers. He thought it was more useful to relegate women to their traditional role within the family. Male workers had to receive wage increases so that men would be in a position to support the whole family without needing their women or children to work. Women's employment was also seen as an element of disaggregation and corruption of the working-class family. Consequently economic considerations were closely tied up with a fundamentally moralistic and conservative mentality. The spread of such ideas within the workers' movement was not only due to sexism and conservatism. One just has to read the description of working-class living conditions in Engels' *The condition of the working class in England* or in Volume 1 of Marx's *Capital* to see the devastating effects of intensive industrial exploitation on the families, lives and bodies of male, female and child workers and to understand how the rejection of female and child labour was also a form of self-defence against this overwhelming exploitation.

After the unification with Bebel's organization which created the German Social Democratic Party, the Lassallian standpoint obviously created lots of problems and additional obstacles for Clara Zetkin's work. She already had to deal with misogynist tendencies within a working class marked by the prejudices of the time. Problems were later caused by the revisionists in the years preceding the First World War at a time when the autonomous women's organizations inside the Social Democratic party and the *Gleichheit* newspaper generally supported clearly revolutionary and anti-imperialist policies. When one adds the fact that it was a woman, Rosa Luxemburg, who was the major theorist of the revolutionary current then we can understand why people took a position against women, their organizations and publications in order to attack revolutionary ideas.

Things were not much better during the Paris Commune despite the fact that Parisian women played an extraordinary, active role. Indeed the question was never raised of extending voting rights to women and in this first experience of class democracy and the construction of a state utterly distinct from that of the bourgeois, we nevertheless saw the exclusion of half the population.

Generally the issue of extending women's suffrage was the subject of fierce debates inside the workers' movement. What people were afraid of was that women, having a more restricted participation in work or society due to their oppression, would perhaps be more conditioned by the influence of religion, superstition and conservative politics. Consequently extending women's suffrage would contribute to the shifting of the political terrain to the right and adversely affect the socialist parties. Historically we see this argument has been regularly dusted off and used. After the victory over fascism in Italy during the Constituent Assembly period, Palmiro Togliatti and a good number of the other Italian Communist Party leadership members would have preferred to avoid the extension of women's suffrage, fearing that it would favour their opponents, the Christian Democrats.

The bogey of the competition of women's labour was also agitated in Great Britain after a promising start which had seen women play a real role in the emerging trade-union movement. The institutionalization of the English trade-union movement, however, brought about the exclusion of women from trade unions for a long period. It was precisely due to this that women-only trade unions and organizations were established, such as the Women's Trade Union League founded in 1874 by Emma Paterson.

2.2 The Stalinist family

Difficulties and contradictions existed from the beginning and the establishment of feminist demands and independent forms of organization were a constant issue of conflict, negotiation resulting in steps forward following by partial setbacks. However, the bureaucratization of the Soviet Union and the victory of Stalinism brought the first real and complete divorce between the workers' movement and women's specific interest and needs. Clara Zetkin, Alexandra Kollontai and Ines Armand had set up an international women's secretariat within the Third International which had been organizationally strengthened after the October revolution. The women's secretariat published a magazine and organized four conferences. After Lenin's death and the onset of bureaucratization, there was a steady elimination or neutralizing of all structures that enjoyed any sort of autonomy. In 1926 the sixth Plenum of the International's Executive Committee decided to dissolve the women's secretariat. The main reason used to justify this decision was now to be used time and time again – separate structures threatened the cohesion of party organizations and of the workers' movement and ran the risk of causing division. This decision was only the start of a long series of measures that within twenty years would result in a complete overturning of all the revolution had succeeded in doing during the early years, in spite of the limits related to the difficult circumstances and the inadequacies of the leadership. In 1929 even the Zhenotdel was wound up, the official reason being that there was no reason for the continuation of an independent women's movement. In the 1930s the official line on the family completely changed. In the first years after the revolution, the family was defined as a place where superstition, prejudice and women's oppression were perpetuated and that would progressively be superseded by the new society. Now it became repackaged in a paternalistic framework.

One of the first measures taken by the October Revolution was the abolition of the "crime" of homosexuality as defined by the Tsarist penal code. Article 121 of the penal code adopted in 1933 re-established homosexuality as a punishable offence with a sentence of five years forced labour, extendable to eight. Furthermore homosexuals were accused of being "objectively" counter-revolutionary and the regime even started to describe homosexuality as a symptom of "fascism". Homosexuality, thanks to this mixing up of political stance and sexual orientation, became an effective tool used in the persecution of dissidents, often without any connection with their real sexual preferences. It was not until 1993 that homosexuality was de-criminalized.

In 1936 the regime turned its attention to women's self-determination. Abortion was already in practice quite difficult to access, now it was banned for the first pregnancy. It was totally banned in 1944. A tax was introduced on single people and the fees incurred in obtaining a divorce were increased. Meanwhile legislation which recognized common-law partnerships was repealed and women were only granted alimony rights when separating if they had been married. A 1944 law forced single mothers to meet the education costs of their children – penalizing them economically and further stigmatizing them. The new inheritance law passed in 1945 strengthened the position of the father as head of the family. Alongside these legal measures all the old patriarchal ideological baggage was wheeled out – condemnation of free sexuality and "sexual perversions", glorification of matrimonial rituals and symbols (ceremonies and rings) and new praise for divided gender roles.

Critics of the October Revolution, not only liberals or conservatives but also some on the left, generally tend to show a line of continuity between the revolution and its bureaucratic degeneration, between Bolshevism and totalitarianism, between

Lenin and Stalin. However, the history of the undisputed changes on the question of women's rights and living conditions, their self-determination, the extent to which the traditional patriarchal family was superseded and the question of sexual freedom, is a valid criteria for verifying the truth of this so-called continuity. For the first generation of Bolshevik leaders the family represented one of the pillars of social order. As they wanted to sweep away the past to open up space for the new, they understood the need to undermine the structure of family. As long as women remained closed within their household walls, under the authority of their husbands, economically dependent and without any possibility of living in non-traditional or non-patriarchal relationships, they would not be able to actively support the creation of a new society. If you wanted to subvert the old order, women's liberation was a necessary step. Obviously this did not mean that there were no contradictions or resistance to change (including within the Bolshevik party) during the first years of the revolution. Errors were made and the male and female Bolshevik leaders did not at that time have a complete theory of women's liberation. Also the pressure exerted by the autonomous women's organizations played a not insignificant role in the process. Nevertheless we cannot deny that women's objective needs and interests coincided to a large extent with those of the revolutionary process.

The traditional family was restored by Stalinism for the very same reasons that the October revolutionaries wanted it to be superseded. It was no longer a question of sweeping away the past, getting rid of the straightjacket of bureaucracy and autocracy or of abolishing exploitation. No, now it was all about guaranteeing the conservation and reproduction of a new bureaucratic caste. Strengthening the family therefore became an important weapon for the Stalinist *Thermidor* insofar as it helped to guarantee what the regime needed – the combination of obedience and productivity. As Trotsky has already pointed out in the *Revolution Betrayed*:

The most compelling motive of the present cult of the family is undoubtedly the need of the bureaucracy for a stable hierarchy of relations, and for the disciplining of youth by means of 40 million points of support for authority and power.

Despite its limits, with the October Revolution women experienced freedoms and a possibility of liberation that bear no comparison with any other country of the time. The experience is still on a different level to that of women in a great part of the world today. There is a huge gap between the ardour of the freedom experienced in the first years of the revolution and the suffocating puritanism of bureaucratic restoration.

2.3 "Trash": communist parties and women

The degeneration of the revolution in the Soviet Union had a decisive influence on all the communist parties belonging to the Third International. Just as with all other policies, the Kremlin laid down the line to be followed. Among the first to pay the costs were Spanish women during the Civil War. From the beginning of the Civil War the Communist Party took a position directly opposed to the Anarchists by putting pressure on Largo Caballero, the Socialist war minister, to liquidate the militia – where women were also fighting – in favour of a solely male, disciplined, regular army. The courage shown by women in the heat of battle was not enough to ensure their right to remain in the front line alongside the men. Caballero did not just dissolve the militia, he also banned women from any combat roles – their place was to be in the rear assigned to productive work. From September 1936 on the elimination of all the organs of dual power that had arisen during the July Days also tended to make the situation worse – it was precisely within these bodies that many women had for the first time the chance to become politically active.

Communist Party policy was channelled though a women's mass organization, *Mujeres antifascistas* (Anti-Fascist Women), set up as the Spanish section of the Third International's

Women against War and Fascism. As the name suggests, the organization was essentially focused on the anti-fascist struggle and was used as a front for the Communist Party, often drawing on women's sense of guilt and responsibility for their children to convince them to give up the idea of fighting alongside men. Obviously this political position was tied up with the general policy of compromise with the bourgeoisie which meant the Communist Party dropped the slogan of a "people in arms" in favour of supporting a regular army. Women's employment was the central question for *Mujeres antifascistas* but at the same time in many official speeches its leaders were quick to stress that women joining the workforce was only a provisional measure. In other words, they were standing in for men involved in the fighting, whose legitimate jobs would be returned to them at the end of the war.

The Communists were not alone in wanting to send women back to the rear. The Partido Obrero de Unificación Marxista (POUM, Workers' Party of Marxist Unification) also decided against women joining the regular army. Furthermore while POUM women had taken up many of the Bolshevik political positions – particularly in relation to dual exploitation and the specific oppression of women, the need to socialize many domestic caring tasks, and equal pay – these policies were mostly absent from the programme adopted at the founding congress in 1935, the 1936 programme and Thirteen Points manifesto of March 1937. As for the Anarchists, while they had much more advanced positions in terms of women's liberation, they still refused to recognize *Mujeres libres* (Free Women) as an official part of the Anarchist movement. The demand for it to be recognized as a sector of the movement was made in 1938 at a regional plenum in Catalonia, but it was rejected with the argument that a specifically feminist organization was a divisive factor for the movement and risked damaging working-class interests.

Some years later, on the other side of the Pyrenees, Simone de Beauvoir's *The Second Sex* was published in 1949 to a nationwide chorus of indignation. Jean Kanapa, an intellectual and member of the Parti communiste français (PCF, French Communist Party) member, added his voice to the outrage by calling the book "disgusting trash". Kanapa's negative reaction was very much in line with the moralizing and "respectable" culture promoted by the PCF – the consequence of bureaucratic degeneration and the 180 degree turn made by the Third International. In France reactionary laws were passed in 1920 and 1923 which banned abortion and contraception. Initially the PCF took a position of outright opposition to these laws and in the 1920s the party sought to organize campaigns to repeal the laws. As a result more women swelled the ranks of the party, including feminists. However in the 1930s the PCF went into reverse gear on these issues and shifted towards almost grotesquely pro-family policies. Support for birth control rights was declared to be a petty-bourgeois deviation. The party made defence of the family one of the key planks of its platform and as an inevitable consequence the women's secretariat was liquidated in 1936. The year before the PCF daily newspaper published an article unambiguously stating "Communists want to inherit a strong country, a multitudinous race."

Contraception and abortion remained taboo subjects for a long time within the ranks of the French workers' movement. The main trade union led by the PCF, the Confédération générale du travail (CGT - General Labour Confederation), refused to include anything about repealing these repressive laws in its own programme even when it chose to defend women's involvement in the labour force. The monthly magazine, *Antoinette*, which it started in 1955, campaigned in defence of women workers as mothers and wives, for example demanding extra time off and pensions at 55 – measures which took into account women's role as mothers and the domestic labour they took on within the family. Contraception and abortion, on the other hand, remained a private matter which women workers had to sort out for themselves. Even the Union of French Women (UFF), the PCF front organization, contributed greatly to this pro-family culture by organizing women mainly as mothers.

In Italy the political stance of the Communist Party on women's questions was strongly influenced not just by the line of the Soviet party but also by the concern of maintaining a good relationship with the Catholic population. The communists were always obsessed with demonstrating that you could be both a religious believer and a party member, for Italy was a country where the Catholic Church exerted great influence and continually intervened in political affairs. In a frenetic attempt to show itself to be more Catholic than the pope, the Partido Comunista Italiano (PCI – Italian Communist Party) went to even more grotesque lengths than the PCF (although less well-known outside the country). Just after the Second World War during the Constituent Assembly phase of the new republic, Togliatti and the other leaders took a clear stand against the idea of introducing the right to divorce – arguing that the country was not mature enough for such "advanced policies". So Italy along with Ireland and fascist Spain were the only countries in Western Europe not to include divorce as a right in their laws.

Official opposition to divorce continued right up to the mid-1960s, when, outflanked on its left by the Partido Socialista Italiano (PSI – Italian Socialist Party) which had put forward a draft law, the PCI leadership finally had to publicly accept the need to also introduce divorce laws in Italy. When the right-wing Christian Democrats launched a referendum to abolish the law, the PCI did everything it could to reach a compromise, proposing a lot of amendments and changes that would have completely nullified divorce rights. The PCI leadership was not only terrified of clearly breaking with Catholic opinion but was also totally convinced that conservative views were going to triumph in the referendum. Enrico Berlinguer, who was Party secretary at the time, confided to Ugo Baudel, a journalist of L'unità, that according to his estimates the pro-divorce side would only get a maximum of 35 per cent of the vote. The 1974 referendum was a clear victory for the supporters of the right to divorce with almost 60 per cent, which showed how out of touch the PCI was with Italian society. We had reached the absurd position where the Communist Party was more conservative, petty-bourgeois and moralizing than society as a whole.

Opposition to divorce was not only dictated by a judgment of the specific context of Italian society but was also informed by a whole vision of gender relations, of the family, of women which meant that divorce was seen as an evil which was only to be used in the last resort. Obviously there was no question of raising the abortion issue. In that period it was still illegal in the Soviet Union – an undisputed model to be followed. For decades the Communist Party had promoted a stifling, paternalistic culture where women were always valued as mothers, daughters or sisters... The family was praised and defended as the cornerstone of society although there were vague mentions of a "different family", supposedly founded on a different basis, which was never really seriously argued for in practice. Even PCI members were victims of this pro-family, petty-bourgeois political line. Activists who split up or showed sexual or romantic behaviour that fell outside this moral austerity were often called into the party offices and asked to justify their private lives and choices. The party's attitude to homosexuality was even more reactionary – for example in the infamous case of Pier Paolo Pasolini's expulsion from the PCI.

The PCI leader Togliatti himself was partially victim of this moralistic and stifling atmosphere in the 1940s. He had separated from his wife Rita Montagnana, who was also a PCI leader and the director of *Noi Donne* (We Women), the newspaper of the Unione Donne Italiane (UDI, Union of Italian Women), a PCI front organization. She had used the pages of *Noi Donne* to intervene against divorce and in support of the family. The relationship between Togliatti and his new partner, Nilde Iotti, met with the disapproval of the party leadership when it met to discuss this very matter. In any case Togliatti only had himself to blame since, along with other leaders, they had issued moral admonishments in every direction, exalting the austere morality of the perfect communist activist, whose family home must be like a glass house – transparent to everybody – while in private their relationships were unstable and far from monogamous. When the relationship between Nilde Iotti and Togliatti became finally officialized, Rita Montagnana was removed from all leadership posts and disappeared from the political scene. The same fate also awaited Luigi Longo's wife, Teresa Noce. One of the most brilliant masters of these double standards was Salvatore Cacciapuoti, party secretary in Naples in the 1940s. As Ermanno Rea recounts in *Mistero napoletano* (Neapolitan Mystery), while he lectured his comrades on their private lives when they contradicted the party's so-called "ethics of the people", Cacciapuoti had no scruples in requesting sexual favours from party members, exploiting his position of authority.

2.4 "Prone"! The divorce of the Seventies

In 1964 Casey Hayden and Mary King, two white activists in one of the main organizations of the American Civil Rights movement, the Student Non-Violent Organizing Committee (SNCC), wrote a document entitled: "Position Paper: Women in the Movement." The document was conceived as a contribution to a SNCC conference to be held in November of that year to discuss the political perspectives and organization of the movement. However, it was not signed by the two militants, for they feared the sarcasm and derision of other activists – particularly since they were two white women. They decided to anonymously slip it into the pile of documents. Hayden and King were certainly not the only white women to participate actively in the civil rights movement. Indeed white women were proportionately more involved than white men. Within the movement white women had finally been able to come into contact with women who differed from the stereotype prevalent among the white American middle classes. They met strong, militant women who played a fundamental role in the struggle for civil rights and whose strength was not ridiculed in their own community. Black women active in the civil rights movement finally provided a role model with whom they could identify and by whom be inspired. Hayden and King's document was one of the first manifestos of women's new radicalization, but it was also one of the first attempts to highlight how even within the civil rights movement the usual male domination was perpetuated just as it ruled in the New Left white-led organizations. "Women in the Movement" started by listing eleven facts or events that showed the persistence of patriarchal organizational attitudes. It highlighted how the sensitivity used to unmask even the apparently insignificant ways that white superiority was assumed was not applied to the reality of gender relations. Women were generally assigned functions and tasks which did not correspond to their personal competence but rather to a sexual division of roles. In this way women invariably ended up doing merely administrative and organizational jobs.

The document is often remembered for the notorious response of Stokely Carmichael, one of the leaders of the movement and among the leading protagonists of the later turn to Black Power and the formation of the Black Panthers: "What is the position of women in the SNCC? The position of women in the SNCC is prone." The comment was made in a break after the meeting and was perhaps intended more as an ironic statement than a serious declaration. But whatever Carmichael meant by it, this revealed the sexist prejudices inside the organization as well as triggering further sexist comments by other members. However the dispute was far from simple. Very few black women were supportive of Hayden and King's document which was interpreted as a symptom of white women's dissatisfaction. They had not managed to assert their own role in the movement not because of sexism but because of racial divisions. In other words at the end of the day they were accused of speaking for white women and of not recognizing the very distinctive leadership role that black women were playing inside the organization.

Things were not much better in the Students for a Democratic Society (SDS), an organization formed in the northern United States among campus students but which sought to attract and organize the urban sub-proletariat and the unemployed. A complete sexual division of political roles was established inside the organization. Women concentrated on questions related to women's living conditions – education, social services, street lighting – and they did this more successfully than men. In this way they succeeded not only in rooting themselves more in society than men but also were able to acquire a greater confidence in themselves and their own strengths. A consequence of this division in the spheres of political intervention was a growing tension inside the organization. SDS men were in daily contact with the most violent, marginal and poorest sectors of society and began to take on their behaviour and outlook, which naturally included deeply sexist attitudes. In a meeting at the University of Washington, a SDS member, explaining how the white university students were building relationships with poor whites, candidly declared that they "all went out together to screw a chick" and that this was a useful form of politicization. The politicization of the "chick" in question was evidently not much taken into consideration. The size and growth of the anti-Vietnam war movement also did not make it any easier for women to take on an important role within it. Since women were not subject to the draft, the focus of the mobilization developing on campuses were men who refused the draft. Women were limited to offering them support.

In 1967 the black movement was still a source of inspiration for feminists. In August the National Conference for New Politics (NCNP) called a national meeting which attracted 2000 activists from about 200 organizations. Black delegates demanded a 50 per cent quota in the commissions and when voting. At that point women delegates also made the same request asking for a quota of 51 per cent as women were 51 per cent of the population. Whilst the demand from the black delegates was in the end accepted, the women's proposals were simply not taken seriously and they were not even allowed speaking time to debate the issue. When five women then tried to occupy the podium to intervene the man chairing the meeting gave one of them a slap saying, "Calm down girl, we have more important things to discuss than women's problems." The girl in question was Shulamith Firestone.

For thousands of American women involved in the civil rights, student or anti-war movements they came up against the same old sexism. The sarcasm, derision and open contempt they were subject to whenever they put forward demands or raised issues concerning their specific oppression as women, led in the end to a sole consequence – the definitive divorce between the feminist movement and other movements.

On the one hand, the anti-war movement declined at the beginning of the 1970s, the student movement disintegrated and Black Power was literally decimated by unprecedented police repression. On the other hand, the American feminist movement was established and grew stronger. The key texts of radical feminism began to be published. One of these was *The Dialectic of Sex* by Shulamith Firestone. Separatist organizations in the United States did not only coincide with a split from the mixed working-class and student organizations, but also from the working class as a whole and therefore from working-class women. The new radical feminism spread essentially among the educated petty bourgeoisie and middle classes, through the emergence of a myriad of small groups which in most cases dedicated themselves to consciousness-raising as women. The focus for activity was shifted to the necessary ways of identifying and then freeing oneself from deep-seated male conditioning. Women's main priority was said to be the analysis of their own personal, family and sexual relationships since it was believed that personal emancipation and transformation was a pre-condition for a more general change.

While in the United States women involved in the movements had to deal with the rampant sexism of the New Left organizations, in Italy and France they found themselves between the devil and the deep blue sea. On the one side they soon discovered, just like their American sisters, that the 1960s and 1970s movements wanted to subvert everything except gender relations. On the other side the French and Italian Communist Parties followed a conservative, rigid political line on everything to do with women's self-determination and freedom. In France three distinct tendencies quickly emerged inside the women's liberation movement. The first, Psychoanalysis and Politics (known as *Psych et Po*) led by Antoinette Fouque based itself generally on psychoanalysis, elaborating a theory founded on an essentialist definition of "difference" derived from women's sexual characteristics. Given this vantage point they refused to identify with the history of feminism. From their point of view feminists, rather than challenging phallocracy, had instead looked to assimilate women to men. *Psych et Po* argued for a separatist politics rejecting any sort of joint action or alliance with men even on questions such as abortion rights. The second current was the materialist feminist one, whose main ideologue was Christine Delphy, which supported the notion of exploitative relations between men and women and saw patriarchy as the main enemy. The third current was "class-struggle feminism" made up mainly of the activists from the mixed trade-union or revolutionary left organizations. In 1972 the Thursday Group decided to break with *Psych et Po* in opposition to the latter's sectarianism and sought to build alliances with the other feminist currents. These conflicts continued throughout the 1970s and exploded when *Psych et Po* unsuccessfully tried to appropriate the MLF name. The debate inside the movement on the type of relations to have or not have with the mixed left organizations was certainly the most lively and complex and remained a factor of division and difficulty within the movement. Feminists coming from mixed organizations but who identified with the class struggle feminists tried over a long period to play a mediating, communicative role between the feminist movement and their organizations. However, to do this they had to deal with sexism and strong resistance within the mixed revolutionary left groups. They had to question their internal functioning, culture and attitudes as well as fighting to integrate a gender perspective within any political analyses that were made. This was not an easy task and ran into generalized opposition as feminism was accused of contributing to the division of the workers' movement and of putting forward a petty-bourgeois political line. It was constantly and lazily defined as petty-bourgeois because of the importance given to the personal sphere and to the coherence between the personal and the political.

In Italy the conflict was even more explosive, firstly because the influence of separatist, radical feminism was much stronger from the start, influencing the later development of the WLM. Secondly because the sexism of the New Left organizations was even more deeply rooted and there was a much more hostile reaction to the growing feminist movement. Carla Lonzi's writings – particularly the manifesto *Sputiamo su Hegel* (We spit on Hegel) – were very much along the same lines as those of the Shulamith Firestone's American radical feminism. They were the founding documents of the new Italian feminism. Her writings completely broke with the history of the workers' movement and its theory. In the glib style of *We Spit on Hegel*, Marx, Engels and Lenin are dismissed as bearers of a profoundly patriarchal, male culture and the precursors of what would become the conservative and anti-feminist politics of the bureaucratized Communist Parties. As Carla Lonzi wrote in the preface to the 1974 edition of *We spit on Hegel* and *Donna Vaginale e Donna clitoridea (Vaginal women and clitorial women):*

I wrote *We Spit on Hegel* because I was very disturbed to see that nearly all Italian feminists gave more credit to the class struggle than to their own oppression. (…) Women themselves seemed to accept being considered 'second rate' if the people doing the convincing were held in esteem by humanity – Marx, Lenin, Freud and all the others.

Carla Lonzi and her group, following the lead of the American feminists, championed the re-discovery of difference – an authentic difference to be found on the existential level more than in politics. They opposed the idea of equality between the sexes, denouncing it as a means of oppression, of annihilating difference and through which women's inferiority was hidden.

Separatist feminism not only criticized any sort of collaboration or alliance with mixed organizations but also any political intervention that reproduced male forms or which involved any sort of compromise with male institutions. For example, on the abortion question Carla Lonzi's group took a distinct position, denouncing abortion as yet another form of violence against women's bodies alongside the innate violence of coitus and of male pleasure. This hostility extended to opposing demostrations held in defence of abortion rights, which were denounced as a male form of political action where feminists accepted to be subordinated to men's politics, while at the same time deluding themselves to believe they were the protagonists.

On the other hand, the New Left's mixed organizations showed they were diametrically opposed to welcoming and accepting the self-organization of the women activists who were fed up of being relegated to the role of "angels of the duplicating machine". Undoubtedly the symbolic expression of this conflict and divorce were the events of December 1975. On 6 December an abortion rights demonstration was called by feminists who wished it to be women only. Lotta Continua, the biggest group on the Italian New Left, decided to not respect the organizers' decision and used its own stewarding force to confront the demonstration's stewards in an attempt to impose a mixed organization on the demonstration where it could display its own party banners and symbols. This incident had an extraordinary impact and aggravated the tensions that already existed inside the organization as a result of the feminist radicalization of its own militants who had already raised issues about its internal functioning. These tensions exploded the following year at the Rimini Congress when the organization, riddled by conflicts between its youth, women and the party security stewards, decided to wind itself up. At the same time other mixed groups, such as "Il Manifesto" also suffered a significant loss of activists due to the breaking out of women who were to join the separatist women's movement.

Similar divisions broke out during the 1977 movement, where a decisive role was played by the autonomous groups. These groups were completely against the self-organization of women who were accused of causing splits inside the working class. During 1977 we saw a number of attacks organized by the autonomous groupings on separatist demonstrations. The first major split happened on 26/27 February at the national coordinating meeting of university students, in Rome. This huge meeting degenerated towards the end into chaos with differences being dealt with through whistling, booing and chanted slogans rather than serious debate. Consequently on 27 February some of the feminist groups decided to leave the meeting denouncing "the appalling climate of violence and abuse that does not allow the views of the movement to be expressed."

In the same year there was a further division inside the feminist movement with the split of lesbians from the feminist committees, denouncing the dominant heterosexual norms within the movement and the difficulty for lesbians to have a visible role. This led to the foundation of the first separate lesbian committees: "Rifiutare" (Refuse), "Artemide" and "Identita negate" (Identity denied) in Rome, "Donne omosessuali" (Lesbian Women) in Milan and "Brigate di Saffo" (Sappho Brigade) in Turin. The growing lesbian movement in many cases pushed separatist organization to the extreme, shifting from an exclusively political level to the sphere of interpersonal relationships. They denounced the contradiction of heterosexual, separatist feminists who, while denouncing patriarchal domination, continued nevertheless to have sexual relationships with men, in this way de facto accepting exploitation and domination.

American radical feminism exerted a significant influence also over the British feminist movement even if the context and the traditional relations between the feminist movement and the workers' movement were rather different from the situation in the United States or in countries with big communist parties. In many ways the feminist movement's demands initially coincided with those of the trade unions and related to the needs of working-class women. Nevertheless as the influence of radical feminism grew so too did the separation of the feminist movement – accentuated by the difficulty of communication between working-class women, organized in trade unions, and the women of the feminist movement who generally had professional "intellectual" jobs. Another factor that probably also weighed, at least in the English context, was a certain resistance by working-class women to the new feminist practice of group consciousness-raising and of discussing the personal. The British feminist movement organized in similar ways to the American one and began to really develop during the 1970 to 1974 period when there were a significant number of workers' struggles. The first body to be set up was the Women's Liberation Workshop, which coordinated a network of small groups. The first National Women's Liberation Conference took place in February 1970 in Oxford, with the 600 women coming for the most part from the local women's liberation groups as well as from the New Left. This conference led to a stable network of women's groups and established a national coordinating committee.

On 6 March 1971 the National Women's Liberation Conference organized women's day marches in London and Liverpool with four key demands: equal pay, equal education and employment opportunities, free contraception and abortion, and 24 hour nurseries. In the following years further demands were added that placed opposition to male domination and its structures of oppression as a focus of the action. The interpersonal relationships at the heart of this domination were raised. In 1975 the National Women's Conference finally added to its list of demands the ending of any discrimination against lesbians and for the right of women to define their own sexuality. In the autumn of 1970 the Gay Liberation Front (GLF) was set up in London and on 28 August 1971 it organized its first demonstration of 2000 people. In 1972 women decided to split from the GLF, denouncing the chauvinist, sexist attitudes of the men inside the organization.

Notwithstanding the now clear divorce between trade unions and the feminist movement, they were still able to collaborate to some degree in the campaign to defend the legal right to abortion launched in 1975 against a proposed amendment to the abortion law which aimed to de facto limit this right without directly attacking the fundamental right to abortion. The campaign organized a mixed demonstration in 1975. The proposed amendment was never adopted but other attacks followed. A second proposed legal change in 1976 tried to reduce the time limit for abortions. Again this time a campaign with thousands of people involved was launched and the counter-reform failed. In 1979, following the election of a Tory government, there was another attempt to weaken abortion rights. This time the Trades Union Congress (TUC) adopted a resolution put forward by the Women's TUC and called a mass demonstration of 80,000 people. This conservative-led attempt to limit abortion rights also failed.

Chapter 3
DANGEROUS LIAISONS BETWEEN GENDER AND CLASS

3.1 Once upon a time ...

Once upon a time were there women? The answer to this question and the question itself are not at all obvious, particularly if we take on what Simone de Beauvoir wrote in *The Second Sex,* that women are not born but become women. This statement was to have a strong influence on the theory of second wave feminism. De Beauvoir wanted to underline the way womanhood was socially, culturally and historically constructed. In other words the "womanhood" or essence of being a woman is the totality of education, prohibitions, normative prescriptions and conditioning that all those destined to be women receive from birth onwards. The "womanhood" of women is then transformed into a naturalized given by the effects of oppression and the exclusion from power and from participation in the cultural sphere, especially production. Since it is men who have historically written, composed music, painted, preached and governed there is no definition of women and what their essence should be that it is not at the same time a product of this male monopoly and the parallel systematic exclusion of women. Women "are" what men have decided they should be in the fantasy world of contradictory but intimately linked definitions: saint and whore, devoted wife and desirable lover, household angel and unfaithful partner, welcoming mother and nagging harpy... All these various positive and negative characteristics attributed to women, who are always thought of as "the other", are functional to their exclusion from power. They are the rotten core which both justifies and conceals oppression through a process of naturalization through which women are nailed to their physiology, becoming prisoners of their uteruses.

In *The Second Sex* Simone De Beauvoir merely states that the systematic exclusion and oppression of women and the consequent creation of "womanhood" by men, has always existed. The basis for this point of view can be found in some key 1950s and 1960s anthropological writings that were to have an important influence on Jacques Lacan and through him on what became Lacanian-inspired feminist theory or "French Feminism". These were works by Claude Lévi-Strauss, particularly *Structural Anthropology* and *Elementary Kinship Structures*. Inspired by Ferdinand de Saussure's structuralist linguistics, he applied it to ethnological studies and developed a theory of the birth of culture based on the invariable and universal structures of exchange. Exchange is in fact the means by which humanity confronts nature and establishes, in opposition to it, culture and thus society. Now, according to Lévi-Strauss, exchange constructs its basic structure through the exchange of women. In other words, society and culture begin where men start exchanging women among themselves – a man receives a woman from another man. This is the framework for his explanation for the incest taboo, insofar as it is only through forbidding sexual relations between blood relatives that you can introduce exogamous relationships and the subsequent exchange of women between different groups. The sexual division of labour is itself a means for creating a state of reciprocal dependency between the sexes in order to guarantee the incest taboo and the regulation of exchange of women. Moreover the latter represents a very clear sense of a structure (in structuralist terms) insofar as it is a universal phenomenon evident in almost all human societies.

What are the consequences of this theory? The first is that in the opposition between nature and culture and in the establishment of society men play an active role while women are limited to being the passive object of the exchange and negotiations between men. Society is therefore created by men and is essentially male. The second consequence is that the subordination of women and the contradiction between masculinity/activity and femininity/ passivity are as old as society itself. On the one hand this has always existed precisely because the establishment of society is essentially the business of men, and on the other hand it represented a transition necessary for the birth of culture in opposition to nature because without the exchange of women this would not have been possible.

Simone de Beauvoir's affirmation that "this has always been a man's world" reflects Lévi-Strauss's thesis according to which the reciprocal ties laid down in matrimony are not between a man and a woman but between men over the allocation of women. Women have always been oppressed, due to their reproductive role, biologically inferior to men because of their continual pregnancies which made them weaker in the face of a hostile natural world and which excluded them from the more creative and prestigious types of work. Lévi-Strauss's thesis, which was far from validated in ethnographic field studies, was later revised and criticized by Lévi-Strauss himself. In later decades it has been overtaken by new developments in anthropological research. Nevertheless it has continued to exert a formidable influence outside of the anthropological field, above all through the application of structuralist methodology and particularly of the structuralist understanding of the incest taboo in psychoanalysis.

In this framework, the response to the question "Were there once upon a time women?", or more clearly "Have there always been women?" is certainly yes, once you define the structure as abstracted from social and historical changes and you present it in its universal and unchanging form. Various theories linked to biology or psychology have been put forward to support the idea that women's oppression has always existed. The reasons examined have been quite diverse – the difference in size and morphology characterizing all primates, men's instinct to take over and control women's reproductive capacity, the aggression and drive for power that supposedly are essential characteristics of men... These types of explanation have been challenged by some anthropologists and sociologists from a Marxist background who start from another research hypothesis – that women's oppression has not always existed but emerged as a result of a complex series of social processes.

The attempt to link the development of male domination to the birth of class society and individual private property and to the overcoming of lineage societies was already made a long time ago by Engels in *The Origin of the Family, Private Property and the State*. Lineage-based societies have a fundamental group of kinship relations which bring together all the descendants of a known common ancestor according to a line of descent that can be either patrilineal or matrilineal. In the first case the line of descent is male and the children belong to the father's clan, while the second is female and the children belong to the mother's clan. In lineage societies, lineage represents the basic social structure and social relations are articulated around kinship lines and relations. For his analysis of lineage societies and marriage relationships Engels to a large extent drew on the work of two writers: Johann Bachofen and his theory of an original matriarchy that was later supplanted by patriarchy, and Henry Morgan, author of *Ancient Society*, a work which established evolutionary anthropology. The scarcity of material available to Engels and the pioneering nature of the ethnographic research at the time, explain many of the factual errors in his book. Engels linked the change in the condition of women and their historical "defeat" to two processes: the progression towards individual private property – against the collective property of the tribe – and the shift from group marriages to marriages between couples. The overturning of matriarchy and matrilineal descent is consequently due to men wanting to ensure the inheritance of their own sons, which necessarily involved the control of women's reproductive capacity and the breaking of the link between women and their kinship group. This reconstruction is based on a myth and on a confused analysis. The myth is that matriarchy existed. In fact it has not been proved and has been directly disputed by the overwhelming majority of modern anthropological researchers. Notwithstanding this, the myth of an original matriarchy has not necessarily played a negative role within the feminist movement, contributing in practice to giving women confidence in themselves and in their own abilities. The confusion arises from not distinguishing between matriarchy and matrilineal descent. The latter does not imply in itself a greater power for women or a more prestigious or important role in society. Despite these errors the method Engels tried to apply to the understanding of the origins and causes of male domination is still useful. In other words it is a question of reformulating this phenomenon within the complex totality of social relations and their evolution, starting from the position that in society before class division matrimonial exchange and kinship relations dominated and structured social relations in general. It is precisely through those relationships that production and distribution relations were articulated and organized within a determined social group. Here the questions raised are still relevant. Were women already living under conditions of subordination in hunter-gatherer societies? What changes in their status took place while the following processes were unfolding: the increase in the production of a surplus; the introduction of horticulture, then agriculture and animal rearing; the emergence of private land ownership and the initial social differentiations within populations?

The anthropologist Eleanor Burke Leacock spent years re-searching in an attempt to show how hunter-gatherer societies were generally characterized by a substantial egalitarianism, not only among the male members of different groups but also between the sexes. Presumably the sexual division of labour was less rigid than has been believed and did not in itself lead to hierarchical relations between the sexes. In her work Leacock shows the determinant role played by the impact of the confrontation with Western colonialists on hunter-gatherer societies. This impact can be measured both on the economic level – destroying the equilibrium that allowed women to control their own labour and production – and the cultural level, introducing a "moral" rigidity in sexual customs and matrimonial relationships that did not exist previously. In the case of the Montagnais-Naskapi people of Labrador, whom Leacock studied in the field, the Jesuit missionaries made a particular effort to introduce previously unknown social values such as the obedience and subordination of the wife to the husband. The collision with colonialism can to a large extent explain why once-egalitarian hunting and gathering societies saw the introduction of hierarchy and domination between the sexes. Moreover the influence of a society where the process of social differentiation was more advanced certainly played a role in the spread of male domination in other societies. However the question is still posed: What is the general cause of the establishment of hierarchical relations between the sexes?

Engels' answer is unsatisfactory, because on the one hand it refers to changes in the social and production relations and on the other hand has recourse to a supposed male instinct to perpetuate his own inheritance and therefore to control women's reproduction. But what are the foundations of this instinct? Is it because of this innate desire to ensure a descendant and the transmission of inheritance to his own sons that men wanted to control women's reproduction, or does this intention to control represent the effect of a more complex totality of phenomenon and processes?

Stephanie Coontz, along with other researchers, has tried to provide a different answer, exploring the connections between matrimonial institutions and production. It was not male control over the women's reproductive capacities but the control of her labour power and of her potential to produce a surplus within a determinate set of production relations and division of labour that explains the transformation of kinship relations and thereby the condition of women. In lineage societies *before* the birth of class society it is in fact the kinship relations that organize the production and distribution of goods on the basis of group or collective property. We can discover the origin of male domination within the transformations that took place in these types of society before the birth of real classes and the emergence of private property and the state. The hierarchy between the sexes and its application to the sexual division of labour are therefore at the origin of the processes of social differentiation that subsequently led to the emergence of classes. The hierarchical relations between the sexes could be said to represent a prototype for the latter.

Where kinship relations organize production the analysis and study of their transformation are fundamental to understanding both women's role in production and the changes to her status. From this point of view the central concept is not matrilineal relations but "matrilocation" because the determinant factor is not the rules of descendence but that of *residence*. In matrilocal societies in fact it is men who have to go and live in their wife's parental home. This means that the product of women's labour remains within her kin or lineage, where the woman generally benefits from collaborative rather than subordinate relationships. The transition from matrilocal to patrilocal arrangements allowed men to expropriate the work and surplus produced by women because moving into the husband's paternal home placed the wife in a context foreign to her where she was deprived of family ties of protection. The product of her labour no longer belonged to her or to her kin but to those of her husband.

The reasons why patrilocality prevailed over matrilocality are varied and the debate remains open. Some researchers support the hypothesis of a conflict with men that women lost. Evidence for this is supposedly seen in the myths existing in different societies that recount a war between men and women or of women reigning over chaos which is overthrown and male order is established. Other writers, such as Stephanie Coontz, support the idea of a complex dynamic process involving different factors from problems over the distribution of the surplus to symbolic and religious roles within the community or to the need to maximize production. Over and beyond these various hypotheses however there is broad agreement about placing the origins of women's oppression in the transition to patrilocality. Men expropriated work done by women and polygamy contributed to social differentiation between men. Having more wives was in fact equivalent to expropriating a bigger quantity of labour power and subsequently accumulating a bigger surplus. Furthermore, the coincidence between production relations and kinship relations led to coincidence between the expropriation of women's labour power and privileged access to and control of their reproductive capacities. In this way economic and sexual oppression overlapped and was mutually embedded.

This type of explanation emphasizes three elements:
1) the fact that women's oppression did not always exist, but rather was linked to the processes of social transformation and transition from the egalitarian lineage societies to class society; 2) the fact that the sexual division of labour was originally less rigid than we had thought and was not in itself a basis for a hierarchy between the sexes. From this point of view the origins of women's oppression should not be sought either in the greater sedentary activity of women compared to men (due to their reproductive role – childbirth, breastfeeding, childcare) or in the lesser importance or prestige of foraging and gathering, food preparation or artisanal production compared to hunting and warfare; and 3) the fact that social and economic factors connected to the production, expropriation and distribution of the surplus and labour power rather than biology are crucial in explaining the origins of women's oppression. The central factor is the type of work that women mostly carry out in these societies – gathering, horticulture and food preparation that makes men much more economically dependent on women's labour than women were dependent on men. Taking control of this labour meant not only ensuring the control of production of subsistence goods but also being able to maximize this production and guaranteeing the accumulation of a surplus.

3.2 Class without gender

What are the consequences of a research hypothesis that tries to seek the origins of women's oppression in a totality of social and economic phenomena, linked to the transition from collectivized or group ownership to private property, the production of surplus and its dynamics of appropriation and distribution and the transition from matrilocality to patrilocality?

If one thinks that women's oppression did not always exist and that its roots are not biological or psychological does it necessarily mean that gender oppression is a secondary oppression, hierarchically subordinated to class exploitation? Does it mean denying its autonomy and specificity? Further, by focusing on only the economic character of oppression does one deny those aspects of male domination linked to the control of women's reproductive capacity, the psychological aspects, the specificity of sexual violence, the autonomy and the durability that patriarchal structures such as the family have acquired? Does it mean reabsorbing gender oppression into class exploitation?

From a theoretical point of view there is no reason to come to this sort of conclusion. However the tendency to create artificial and unhelpful hierarchies of oppressions and exploitations rather than understanding the reciprocal interconnections has always been present in the workers' movement. This tendency thought that the ending of capitalism would lead naturally and automatically to the emancipation of women and also saw the autonomous organization of women as a threat to class unity – a unity that was supposed to magically resolve women's issues. This ideology contributed in a decisive way to the worker's movement divorce with feminism. Engels' optimism over how women's joining the labour force would be the key to their emancipation has been disproved by reality itself.

This certainly does not mean that Engels was wrong to emphasize the fundamental importance of women's economic independence, which is one irrefutable condition of their liberation. No one can deny that the increase in female employment in the last hundred years has changed women's lives in a substantial way, indeed it has transformed the forms in which gender oppression is articulated. Nevertheless patriarchal structures have proved to be much more resistant and durable than foreseen. Even the obvious, bitter evidence before our eyes of the ongoing oppression of women in post-capitalist societies (from the Soviet Bloc to Cuba...) should teach us something and raise some serious questions. Privatizing the sphere of reproduction – that is all those activities that guarantee the physical, mental and emotional reproduction of labour power (eating, sleeping, dressing, washing, relaxing...) which is encouraged and used by capitalism, has given enormous power to family ties and makes the socialization of these reproductive functions difficult to imagine and even more difficult to get accepted.

One just has to think of the resistance often put up to attempts during revolutionary periods to free women from the caring role by transferring it outside of the family through the setting up of canteens, laundries and communal nurseries. The opposition between public society and the private sphere has developed around the demarcation that separates the family, the private space par excellence, from the state, society and the market. Therefore the family has become the space – often more imaginary than real – where one's true self is expressed in opposition to the external world of exploitation, alienation, brutalization, aggression and competition. A place where affection and sentiment, that are impossible in the external world, can blossom. Already in the *1844 Economic and Philosophical Manuscripts* Marx had a basic understanding of this particular framing of relationships brought about by capitalism:

> As a result, therefore, man (the worker) only feels himself freely active in his animal functions – eating, drinking, procreating, or at most in his dwelling and in dressing-up, etc; and in his human functions he no longer feels himself to be anything but an animal. What is animal becomes human and what is human becomes animal.

Certainly eating, drinking, procreating, etc., are also genuinely human functions. But taken abstractly, separated from the sphere of all other human activity and turned into sole and ultimate ends, they are animal functions.

In the context of this shake up of human relations the family structure has ceased to be a unit of production (except for some sectors of production such as family-based agriculture) and has been relegated to a private space rigidly separate from the public sphere. It has lost one function but has acquired another that gives it a particular power. It would be – and already has been – a massive error to underestimate its ideological nature and the scale of the psychological attachment to this structure and to its dynamics, including the role women have within it insofar as they carry out the majority if not the totality of the reproductive functions. To have thought that the class struggle alone could resolve this question, magically dissolving family ties and radically changing its character without an adequate analysis of the problem, without challenging sexual roles and without a specific politicization of women is in the best of cases to be blinded by optimism, and in the worst of cases to show utter bad faith.

The same point can be made in relation to the underestimation of the effects of gender and its hierarchical relations on the working class and its politicization. Considering the working class only in its masculine form means in the first place to fail to grasp or to grasp only partially the way in which the relations of production and exploitation function and are structured and therefore not to understand or to only partially understand how capitalism works. Secondly it results in failing to understand how gender oppression provides a powerful weapon to divide the working class, to create hierarchies within it and to ideologically control it. It is the same blindness that has led the workers' movement over the long term to be unable to deal with racist or ethnic repression and to fail to provide a satisfactory analysis or political approach.

3.3 Gender as class

While the perspective of a genderless class was one of the main limits of the bulk of the workers' movement and of the Marxist tradition, materialist and "wages for housework" feminism have attempted to rethink the relationship between class and gender from a radically different point of view: that of gender as class.

The analyses made in the 1970s by theorists such as Christine Delphy, the founder of materialist feminism, from France, and the Italian thinkers Alisa Del Re and Mariarosa Dalla Costa, who are among the main exponents of "wages for housework" feminism, overlap on some ideas about the nature of female domestic labour inside the family. Both tendencies talk about the exploitation of women's reproductive work, which is assigned a productive character in Marxist terms. Contrary to orthodox Marxist positions, which are accused of undervaluing the function of reproductive labour and denying its productive role, this interpretation argues domestic labour produces commodities and surplus value. It is a question of productive labour for which women are not paid. Consequently the distinction between oppression (applied to women) and exploitation (applied to classes and class relations) has no sense, to the extent that women are not just oppressed but are exploited, in other words their work produces surplus value which is appropriated by someone else.

In fact for "wages for housework" feminists when Marx in *Capital* states that the value of the commodities necessary for a worker's reproduction is contained in labour power value (clothing, food, housing...) he does not take into consideration another value – the work of caring which is necessary for the functionality of labour commodity value. As Christine Delphy writes, if you follow Marx's analysis here it would mean pork and potatoes with their skins intact would be consumed raw after their production and purchase. Between the production or purchase of the pork and potato commodities and their consumption you have their preparation and cooking which transform these commodities into a usable form. In the same way one presumes that clothes, as well as being bought and worn also have to be periodically washed, ironed and mended. Materialist and "wages for housework" feminism criticize Marxism from not considering this work that takes place within the isolated family home as productive labour. To make their point that we are dealing with productive labour and not just use value, as claimed by orthodox Marxists, both these currents use the examples of how a series of domestic labour services are clearly produced and exchanged as commodities. Indeed a meal can be prepared at home but it can also certainly be consumed ready to eat in a restaurant – in this case the value connected to the preparation is added to the commodity value of the food. The same thing applies to laundry services, cleaning, the care of children carried out in the nursery or by babysitters and also for looking after old or ill people. The fact that all these series of services, when not being carried out inside the family home, can be produced and exchanged as commodities, demonstrates that nothing can justify defining the work that women carry out inside the home as being non-productive labour. The only reason for it to be considered in this way is that it is not paid – the unpaid or apparent "free" aspect of it covers up its real character.

The analogy between "wages for housework" feminism and materialist feminism ends at this point – the conclusions that are drawn from considering domestic labour as productive are diametrically opposed. For the "wages for housework" feminists it is capitalism that has transformed the family's role and structure, creating the nuclear family in such a way as to deny its role as a productive unit and relegating women to a subordinate position reproducing labour power. Capitalism has tended to exclude women from production apart from inside the family and assigns men a wage sufficient to maintain himself and his wife and family, absolving itself of any responsibility for the economic survival of the whole family and in this way ensuring that the much more costly work of reproducing labour power is done solely by women inside the family home. Completely socializing this work would incur costs and technological investment much higher than those involved in women's domestic labour. In this way the labour contract between the capitalist and the worker as the "head of the family" in a sense also includes the other members of the family. At one and the same time there is a labour contract and a "sexual contract" which gives men free access to women's bodies and their children. Through this contract unpaid slaves (housewives and any women who carry out domestic labour) are used to reproduce wage slavery (both male and female workers) and women become an integral part of the working class, even if they are not formally hired as employees. Just like their husbands, sons and fathers they suffer from capitalist exploitation and produce surplus value, producing the commodity of labour power. This is the basis on which "wages for housework" feminists prioritize the demand for wages for housework so that the work of reproducing labour power is fully recognized as productive labour and ceases to be an indirect retribution through the husband's salary.

Delphy's conclusions are more or less in direct contradiction to this. Contrary to the "wages for housework" feminists, Christine Delphy argues that it is not capitalism that appropriates domestic labour, even if it certainly benefits from it, but rather men themselves. The direct beneficiary of women's productive/reproductive work is her male relation (husband, father, brother) or partner. Alongside the capitalist mode of production there is another one, which is generally not recognized as such – the patriarchal mode of production. The latter determines the production relations between men and women and is based on the total appropriation by men of women's domestic labour. Men and women form two antagonistic classes within production relations that are based on an exploitative relationship where men profit from women's work. From this point of view, seeing women as belonging to the husband's social class simply arises from uncritically assuming a patriarchal position, tending to cover up the relations of exploitation and subordination which place men in opposition to women. All women are members of the same class and undergo the same exploitation, as a consequence of domestic labour, which can take on very different forms depending on their father or husband's class, whether it is Bill Gates or a shop worker. Capitalism certainly contributes to the maintenance of the patriarchal mode of production through its mechanisms excluding women from production and establishing hierarchies of labour. Given that women are discriminated against through inheritance and property laws, and are either excluded from the labour market, constantly threatened with redundancies (for example they are usually the first to lose their jobs at times of crisis) or underpaid, the only solution they are offered is often marriage. However when marrying they enter into a sort of contract of servitude with men because they exchange their own labour for their husband's control of their maintenance rather than a salary. It is exactly the same way in which slavery operates.

The political consequences of these two approaches to the question of domestic labour and of women's role in the family are obviously very different. In the first case what is emphasized is the way women undergo the same exploitation as men and therefore share a common enemy with them – capitalism. Working-class housewives are full members of their class because they carry out productive labour that is absolutely central for the social reproduction of capital and contributes to creating commodity value and has a very specific role within the capitalist division of labour. This approach, while correctly pointing out the gaps in Marxist theory with respect to the analyses of the role of labour in reproducing labour power and while correctly emphasizing the centrality of this aspect for a full understanding of the mechanisms of capital's functioning and social reproduction, has pushed its logic too far so that it ends up with a rather ineffective political position. Obviously the labour of reproduction indirectly contributes to the producing commodity value. Male or female workers produce commodities – whether visible or invisible – expending mental, physical and emotional energies that have to be regenerated. If these energies are not regenerated then labour power cannot be sold as a commodity and therefore cannot produce surplus value. From this point of view the fact that chapter 7 of *Capital Volume 1* does not directly deal with the question of domestic labour within its analyses of the reproduction of labour power and its value, does leave open a significant problem. Nevertheless to claim that domestic labour produces surplus value means overlooking what must be the essential point for understanding the nature and the way in which capitalism has transformed the family. The fundamental point in fact is that this work of reproduction takes place *outside* of the capitalist market, in isolation which makes it impossible to talk of average socially necessary labour because this labour is neither formally or informally hired under capitalism. In this sense it is difficult to talk about the production of surplus value precisely because, on the one hand, capitalism has taken the function of a unit of production away from the family and, on the other, has ensured that the work of reproducing labour power takes place mostly inside the family, relegating it to a sort of limbo separated from the process of production and circulation of commodities.

This particular aspect has been largely ignored by Christine Delphy, as if the question is about the *nature* of the services offered by the work of caring rather than their location within the context of the process of production and circulation of commodities. Clearly cooking or cleaning in themselves are services that can be sold as commodities and that it is nothing to do with their *nature* which justifies the fact that they are offered freely. Surely the point is that within the family these services are offered freely and are therefore taken out of the sphere of exchange and are not produced or exchanged as commodities. A commodity is a *thing* but what makes it a commodity is not the physical nature of the thing – whether it is a pear or software is unimportant – but its social *form* – how is it produced and consumed.

Insisting on the productive character of domestic labour

has certainly highlighted its importance against its previous undervaluation and can provide a degree of "effective" explanation. The problem is that in both cases it creates analytical confusion that has political consequences. In the first case the logical conclusion is that this work should be paid and the political demand that flows from it is that of wages for housework. However this demand far from challenging the sexual division of labour actually reinforces it – contributing to keeping women inside the family home and therefore isolating them from production and a broader social life. Furthermore proposing wages for housework was understood as a payment for the production of a commodity (that is, labour power). In reality the housewife's work remains within the sector of the reproduction of the conditions that allow labour power to be present on the market as a commodity. Therefore rather than talking about wages we should talk about an income or return (equivalent to a return on investment or property). From this point of view we can see some continuity in the "post-worker" theorists who put forward the idea of a citizen's basic or living income. The same problem arises – proposals for a citizen's income does not in fact threaten the basic mechanisms of capitalist exploitation and does not challenge production relations.

In the second case the major political consequence arises from the presupposition of the existence of production relations different from capitalist ones and based on the sexual division of labour within the family. The logical conclusion of this position is the idea that a defined class, women, exists whether they are wives of industrial magnates or the very poorest and they are in an antagonistic relationship with a male class of exploiters. The political consequences of this approach are outlined by Delphy herself in *The Main Enemy* (L'ennemi principal). While capitalism contributes in a determinant way to sustaining the "patriarchal mode of production" and therefore most be fought, the "main enemy" of women nevertheless is patriarchy. From this point of view it is necessary:

1)   To campaign aggressively on the question of "false consciousness" – that is a class consciousness determined by belonging to a class within the capitalist mode of production which means that women identify with the antagonistic patriarchal class (i.e. their husband's class) instead of developing a true consciousness of the women's class determined by the patriarchal mode of production.

2)   To demonstrate how this false consciousness is harmful to the struggle against patriarchy and serves the latter's interests.

In other words, in the first instance women must stop identifying with the basic capitalist classes (the working class and the bourgeoisie) in order to become conscious of their class position within patriarchy and therefore their solidarity of interests as women.

Such an approach pre-supposes that the housewife of a petrochemical worker, forced to juggle final demand bills, having rent to pay and lung cancer that is probably destroying the health of her husband, has more material interests in common with the of Bill Gates' wife than with her own husband insofar as she shares the same relations of servitude toward her husband. Obviously it is true that women's oppression is transversal and involves all social classes. As far as possible therefore it is correct to envisage working for all women organizing around common interests concerning women's self-determination, their sexuality and their bodies. However there is a real difference between this position and thinking that women's oppression takes the same form irrespective of one's class position; that the determination of one's class by where a woman lives and works (or does not work) or whether she is a captain of industry is simply a question of false consciousness and not the sharing of certain material interests. It does not imply in the end that the strategy needed to respond to her own oppression is always the same for all women. Furthermore, Christine Delphy has often emphasized the fact that it was not her intention to analyse the entire reality of women's oppression but only its economic aspect. However, once the relations between men and women are defined in terms of "slavery" it is a little difficult to understand how this does not over-determine the other areas of life – what type of affection, sexuality, relationships and alliances is it possible to have between a slave and her master?

Both materialist feminism and the wages for housework version have highlighted some fundamental aspects of domestic labour, but their theoretical approach, taken as a whole, risks being nothing but the reverse reflection of the way in which the role of reproduction and women's oppression was not considered to be important by a good part of the workers' movement. Since for the latter the main political focus is the class, then these feminist authors try to transform gender into class. The result is the same, from opposed points of view: gender is reduced to class, in the first case to the working class, in the other to a patriarchal class created ad hoc. In this way the sphere of reproduction is submerged into production, thereby losing its very specificity.

However a doubt remains whether another approach could be possible, an approach that does not renounce the categories of the critique of political economy, understanding nevertheless not only that these categories are not sufficient to grasp the reality of gender, but that it is not possible or useful to apply them in a mechanical way.

3.4. Gender without class

"Wages for housework" feminism and materialist feminism have not been the only way of tackling the questions of reproduction and sexuality within the feminist theory of the second wave. On the contrary, within the maelstrom of currents, threads and publications that emerged with the new flowering of feminist thought the questions of reproduction, sex and sexuality have emphatically occupied centre stage – even if the nebulous nature of the movement makes it very difficult to define or reconstruct definitions, labels, genealogies and intellectual affinities. Demanding the politicization of sex and sexuality as opposed to the centrality of production and class relations was a formative element in the feminist split from the mixed social movements in the 1970s. However the ways in which sex, sexuality and then gender had erupted into political discourse took many different paths which were often very diverse. Within this proliferation of theoretical proposals, which had variable links with collective political action (from the absence of any links to attempts at total absorption), psychoanalysis was one of the main players. It was a negative interlocutor for currents and thinkers who had wanted to unmask its fundamental misogyny, questioning the Oedipus complex theory and that of penis envy as explanations for the formation of sexual identities. On the other hand through a process of assimilation, modifications and sometimes real misunderstanding it was a gold mine, particularly in its Lacanian version, for other currents.

In the same way the interpretations of the term "gender", suggested again by a paper written in 1974 by Gayle S. Rubin, *The Exchange of Women. Notes on the political economy of Sex,* were very diverse. Rubin's paper proposed a distinction should be made between the two concepts of "sex" and "gender". While the former, according to Rubin, indicated biological and anatomical sexual difference between men and women, the latter is the result of a historical, social and cultural construction. The difference related to gender, and not sex, is claimed to be the seedbed of hierarchy and subordination and therefore is the enemy that has to be fought. Over the course of the last thirty years the nature of gender and its significance, its relationship with sex and sexuality, have been the subject of intense debate, which also in this case has led to diverse conclusions.

Radical feminism emerged first in the United States towards the end of the 1960s. What the various theories of this current share, over and beyond any differences, can be understood by the demand encapsulated in its very name. It is a question of directly confronting the "roots" [roots = radix, radic– in Latin, translator's note] of women's oppression, of opposing patriarchy head on. Patriarchy is understood as an autonomous system of oppression by men and is defined as the main enemy. In this way radical feminists differentiate themselves from both liberal feminists and socialist feminists. To fight their oppression women must equip themselves with their own interpretation of the world, rejecting any existing ideologies since they are a result of male supremacy and define their own political line that puts women's interests at the centre in opposition to male interests. Within the patriarchal system all women suffer oppression by all men, all men benefit from the subordination of women and all the other forms of exploitation, hierarchy and supremacy are only the extensions of male supremacy. Patriarchy, therefore, pre-dating capitalism, racism and colonialism represents women's principal, common enemy. As Kate Millet argues in *Sexual Politics* (1970) sexual oppression is not only a form of political domination but it is the first form of domination, preceding all others and must therefore be fought before the others.

In *The Dialectics of Sex: The Case for Feminist Revolution,* a work written in the same year, Shulamith Firestone identified the biological difference between men and women as the roots of female subordination. Nature has clearly placed women in a position of weakness compared to men, assigning her a reproductive role that once pregnancy and birth is over means women have to take care of the baby and breastfeed which are physical duties and conditions putting her into a situation of insecurity and difficulty, necessarily requiring male protection. While nature made women into slaves that does not mean that this slavery is her unchanging destiny. On the contrary, the possibility of separating sexuality from procreation, liberation from compulsory heterosexuality, and socialization of childcare made possible by culture, science and technology, represent the key to women's liberation. By identifying nature, biological and anatomical differences as the roots of women's oppression, Firestone rejects both the Marxist explanation that relates it to the more general process of social differentiation and to the emergence of private property and also the psychoanalytic thesis.

Criticism of psychoanalysis was one of the battle cries of a substantial number of radical feminists. They had subjected it to a similar critical analysis aimed at unveiling the misogynist or sexist nature of various forms of cultural, artistic, philosophical and literary expression, which are inevitably sexist because men had historically monopolized culture. Psychoanalysis was attacked for having provided a naturalistic and therefore tendentially unchangeable vision of how a hierarchy was formed within the process of the formation of gender identity, through the theory of the Oedipus complex, penis envy and the castration complex. Indeed, according to Freud, in the first years of infancy babies of both sexes share the same object of desire – the love of the mother and the same sexuality, oral then anal and initially also phallic. Both sexes in fact see themselves having a penis given that the baby girl sees her own clitoris as a penis. Through reciprocal exploration the children at a certain point realize their own anatomical differences and the male child sees the absence of a penis on the girl child's body as the confirmation of his own fear of castration. In this reciprocal recognition the male child carries out a negative evaluation of the imperfect anatomy of the female child, while the latter for her part develops envy for the penis she does not have. From that moment the pathways diverge. The male child is pushed to be freed up from the Oedipus complex – that is the competition with his father for the mother's love – for fear of implicit castration as a threat if the incest taboo was broken. Law, represented by the social figure of the father, finds a positive structural effect in him, which contributes to the breaking of Oedipal bonds, drawing on the castration threat. The female child on the other hand has quite a different journey. She discovers her anatomical incompleteness and is pushed to abandon her mother as an object of love insofar as the latter does not have a penis and shares with her daughter the same biological privation and consequently has to deflect the father's desire. She goes into the Oedipal complex at the time she recognizes her own anatomical incompleteness and the incest taboo is less effective with her since the threat of castration carries no weight since the female child is already castrated. The Oedipal ties with a paternal father that represents Law at the same time are never completely broken which has a series of consequences for the structure of the women's personality: dependence on authority, little social interests and the unfulfilled request for privileges to compensate for the lack of a penis ...

Now it is rather clear why this interpretation of the formation of sexual identity and its differentiation have been bitterly criticized by many feminists. Firstly, it considers the woman's body as anatomically lacking something insofar as it does not have a penis. Secondly, it attributes to women a series of natural characteristics that is supposed to explain their specific role within society rather than being seen as the effects of the role women have historically been assigned – getting the causes and effects totally the wrong way around which is typical of ideology. Thirdly, it interprets these characteristics as something invariable, to the extent that they are embedded in the process of structuring of the identity determined by symbolic (and therefore pre-social) figures of the mother and father. Finally, the very rigidity and invariability of the symbolic mother and father figures, their identification with social beings (the mother and father in the flesh) and therefore reading the structuring of sexual and gender identity around the male/female dichotomy and heterosexual desire so that both homosexuality and other forms of sexual identity are supposed to represent pathologies.

Alongside these criticisms Anne Koedt adds another in her article published in 1970, *The Myth of the Vaginal Orgasm*. In this work, Koedt, basing herself on a number of studies that demonstrated that the only sexual female organ able to produce an orgasm is the clitoris, dismantles the Freudian idea of the transition from clitoral orgasms to vaginal ones as being a process of maturing as women as a way of freeing her – but only partially – from penis envy and thereby allowing her to emerge from an adolescent phase.

On the other hand, psychoanalysis has fared quite differently in another current of feminist thought known as the feminism of difference or "French feminism" according to a definition that emerged in reality in the United States (so identifying it in geographical terms makes little sense). The idea of difference is central for radical feminism and in fact is of key importance as a conceptual justification for "splitting" from the social movements through the assertion of women's difference. However this takes on a different significance in "French feminism", whose main theorists, Luce Irigaray, Julia Kristeva and Helene Cixous, have refused and even criticized the notion of "feminist" and have had very little connection with the feminist movements, particularly in France. Both Irigaray and Kristeva studied with Jacques Lacan and have a close but critical relationship with his ideas. Lacan had introduced an important amendment to Freud's theory of penis envy, preferring to define it as phallic envy where the phallus essentially signifies power. The female baby therefore does not envy the male reproductive organ but the phallus as the signifier of authority, of the access to the symbolic order and faculty of speaking from all of which she is excluded. Recognition that she does not have a phallus is equivalent to internalizing this exclusion from the symbolic order. This castration mechanism, linked to an historicization of the phallus and its role as a signifier of power, is potentially productive for an understanding of the psychological consequences that oppression has for women and the way in which subordination, with its trappings of insecurity and masochism, is internalized. However, what must be avoided is to enclose the phallus in the symbolic and pre-social realms, thereby making this and the exclusion from it, the cause of women's subordination rather than seeing how the identification between the authority signifier and the penis is the effect of a pre-existing hierarchy between the sexes which has quite different causes.

On the contrary, Irigaray and Kristeva's trajectory is quite different - they essentialize sexual difference. Irigaray takes up and indirectly criticizes Lacan's "mirror" concept developed by the psychoanalyst in his paper *Le stade du miroir* (The Mirror

Stage). For both baby girls and boys seeing themselves reflected in the mirror for the first time is a key experience in the process of construction of their identity insofar as seeing their own image in the mirror initiates the perception of themselves as separate from their mothers. After that we have the imposition of the symbolic order of the Father who lays down the distinction between masculinity and femininity, assigning them particular roles. Irigaray counterposes the speculum to the flat surface of the mirror that reflects external visible images. The speculum is a concave optical instrument used in medicine to look inside human orifices. Women function as mirrors for men because male superiority is reflected in the inferiority of women. Men therefore see women in reference to themselves, as their own opposites, the own inverted images, she is deprived of what he has – the phallus. In this way the woman becomes empty, an absence the male phallus has to fill. Whereas the speculum allows one to look inside and to see that the female genital organs are not simply lacking something, an emptiness to be filled by the phallus, but on the contrary have a much greater sexual richness than the male. This richness becomes unrecognizable in men's phallocentric discourse insofar as they are afraid of sexual difference and need to see their own inverted image in the female and nothing more. The natural consequence of this perspective is the affirmation of the rediscovery of a difference that although already existing has to be rediscovered and re-interrogated after having been for so long suffocated; a difference that has its roots in biology, the difference between male and female reproductive organs.

Julia Kristeva carries out a different type of theoretical operation with Lacan but, all things considered, uses the same method as Irigaray – giving value to what has been historically undervalued, changing a negative sign into a positive one. In this case Kristeva concentrates on the pre-oedipal phase, preceding the imposition of the Father's symbolic order, the origins of language. She defines this period as the "semiotic order" – the order of signs. The semiotic order is that of the mother and represents the period of the exclusive relationship between the baby and its mother before the separation carried out by the father through the threat of castration. Kristeva's intentions are to highlight the role of this pre-oedipal phase, generally undervalued by psychoanalysts, within the process of the formation of the subject. In this phase communication between mothers and babies takes place essentially through gestures (caresses, bodily contact and general care) rather than words. The coming of the Father's symbolic order and thereby language strangles the semiotic order that nevertheless never entirely disappears given that what is repressed is never eliminated. The real task is to try and rediscover and speak about everything that male conceptualization and language have suffocated and to talk about the mother's semiotic order just as artists and poets transgress the symbolic order through rebelling against its laws.

Irigaray and Kristeva became the fundamental reference point for many theorists of "French feminism" such as Luisa Muraro, who developed the idea of sexual difference in an organic vision based on the necessity for women to build a symbolic feminine order in her book *L'ordine simbolico della madre* [The mother's symbolic order, 1997]. In a similar vein, Adriana Caverero wrote *Per una teoria della differenza sessuale* [For a theory of sexual difference, 1987] and is a supporter of the possibility of constructing a language that gives a voice to sexual difference – refusing the monolithic imperialism of male language, which tries to absorb and assimilate the Other to himself. The conditions of women's separation in this way becomes an opportunity to rediscover and research difference and the confiscated Other.

This binary logic of difference was challenged in the 1980s in the theoretical developments of Lesbian feminism. Monique Wittig, for example, who comes from the materialist feminist current, wrote a paper in 1980, *One is not Born a Woman* where she rejects the definition of lesbians as women. Women and men in fact represent two antagonistic classes and heterosexuality is a norm established to sustain the division into sexual classes, reproducing the conditions for the exploitation of women. Lesbians are not women because they break the heterosexual contract, they are fugitives from the classes to which they have been assigned. They are therefore "non-women" and their conditions open the way to the liberation of all other women. Generally lesbian thinkers have come to challenge the binary concept of "women" and "men", attempting to put forward a rethinking of sexuality, sexual identity, sex and gender. Queer theory, developed in the 1990s, particularly with Judith Butler's work, has more than anything else advanced the challenge to gender identity and its connection to sexuality. Perhaps Butler's greatest contribution has been the introduction of the concept of gender as "performative" – being constructed through the repetition of stylized acts in time that she particularly elaborated in *Gender Trouble* and *Bodies that Matter*. She attempts to provide a theoretical alternative both to conceiving difference as an ontological essence and social constructivism. Both positions, according to Butler, endanger the possibility of free subjective action through a determinism which in the first case eliminates it from the inside either through determined sexual or biological identity or through the symbolic process of identity formation or through both together. In the second case the restriction comes from the outside, through the social construction of gender as a given reality to which one submits. Conceptualizing gender as a "performance" means not considering it as something static, already set once and for all, but rather as a totality of acts, gestures and behaviours that represent "gender discipline" and which continually create gender identity. According to the classical inversion of cause and effect there is the tendency to understand the actions and behaviours that distinguish one gender from another as being the product of an already defined identity, of a subject that is already "gendered". But it is precisely the opposite – it is these actions and behaviours that "perform" gender, as regulatory rituals that tend to be continually repeated, that define who is a woman and who is a man and which end up even shaping the body materially. Power relations in fact form the body, disciplining, shaping and sexualizing it to conform with gender. Thus the body is constructed by discourse to the point that some bodies – those of transsexuals for example – do not count and have no right to existence or expression in the discourse. Further radicalizing Foucault, Butler in this way extends the process of dissolution of the subject to the point that the body itself is no longer a core subjective identity but rather the product of extensive power relations.

In order to exist, gender needs to continually repeat those actions that form it – it is nothing without this continual rehearsal which, far from being contingent, is under constant regulation. Continually "making" gender also at the same time "undoes" gender in the sense that, in constantly performing the gender process through acts that fit with codes of behaviour, cracks, contradictions and fissures continually occur. This breakdown in the performance opens up the possibility for the subject to undo gender and thus for its possible subversion.

Radical feminism, theories of difference and queer theory put forward divergent visions of gender, sex and sexuality although they do have some points in common. What they generally do have in common is a radical shift in attention towards the level of discourse and language as the place for defining gender identity and forming a hierarchy between the sexes. Using deconstruction methods they have either revealed the misogynist character of many cultural products or analysed the linguistic lapses or stammering that point back to the repressed, to the Other who is not allowed to speak. The attention given here to the ideological character of gender oppression and its psychological implications has certainly filled a gap in the study of women's oppression, but at the cost of often reducing the complexity of reality to the level of language and discourse and making psychoanalysis the key to understanding everything. Both radical feminists and difference theorists ("French feminists"), albeit for different aims and objectives, have contributed to the dehistoricization of the relations of oppression between the sexes.

Seeking the roots of patriarchy in the biological differences between men and women, as for example Firestone does, and to claim therein lie the origins of male supremacy, which is then extended to other spheres and creates other equivalent systems of domination and oppression, is the exact reversal of the orthodox Marxist method which aims to show that women's oppression is simply derived from class exploitation. It also means making patriarchy into something static and invariable as if the forms of gender oppression and the role it plays are historically always the same and uniform throughout the world. The separatist choice, which in most cases goes hand in hand with calling for the struggle against patriarchy to be the primary one as opposed to all others and with defining men and women as antagonistic classes, has hardly contributed to building an effective women's political perspective. In fact it has rather contributed to the feminist movement's isolation and closure pushing it exclusively towards cultural and ideological critiques, more or less systematically and rapidly steering it away from the question of social alliances. This state of affairs was further aggravated by the extreme fragmentation – including on a theoretical level – of the movement into various components – heterosexual, lesbian, black, black lesbians...

The split from the workers' and social movements is accompanied by the obliteration of any critique of the relations of production which are replaced by relations of power and domination in the wake of post-modernist tendencies, particularly inspired by Foucault's ideas. Consequently they tend to concentrate exclusively on the institutions that guarantee and maintain the system of sexual roles – matrimony, the family, prostitution and heteronormativity. The positive understanding that relations of sexual oppression are political relations is not linked to a criticism of class relations with which patriarchal oppression is inevitably articulated, nor of production relations where they are embedded. Inevitably this has political and theoretical consequences. Firstly, the difficulty in understanding how other factors such as class and race have an influence not only on the forms of oppression suffered but also on the processes of women's identification and subjectivity. Conflicts arose quite quickly as they came up against black women in the liberation movements who refused to put their class or racial identity into the background below their female identity. It led to black feminists splitting away. Often an idealist or purely psychological reading was given of the roots of male domination. For example, the New York Radical Feminist group claimed that men wanted to dominate women not so much for a material benefit but to satisfy their own egos. One thing is not underestimating the psychological dimension of oppression and the relative psychological benefits enjoyed by those who oppress, but it is quite another thing to think the satisfaction of the ego can be the cause of an entire system of domination.

Some tendencies of radical feminism in fact have gone so far in their criticism of men in the sexual area that they have arrived at a position that stands alongside – through a sort of coincidence of the opposites – moralists or even reactionaries. This is the case for example with the group Women against Pornography and of writers and activists like Catharine McKinnon and Andrea Dworkin, who in the 1980s ended up promoting a campaign in favour of a law to ban pornography as a form of sexual discrimination (a law that was later adopted in various states in the USA and Canada). In this way they helped strengthen political and state control over sexuality, giving it a big progressive gloss. So people could now just bring in the struggle against sexual discrimination when raising the question of offending public morality.

By a strange convergence some proposals by the sexual difference theorists also come dangerously close to moralizing or conservative positions on sexuality. In the *Temps de la Différence* [Time of difference], Luce Irigaray is in favour of a law on virginity which gives a special status to girls who decide to keep their virginity as long as they want, without undergoing pressure from men. A virginity law providing a reference point on this question would supposedly in this way help young women have an autonomous, positive identity. An officially recognized virginity status would be a precondition for loving relations with the opposite sex to be really free. It appears to be difficult for Irigaray to consider that young women can develop a positive identity that does not depend on whether their hymen is intact. Once again, women are reduced to their bodies and their sexual organs. It is not an arbitrary proposal, in fact it is the natural consequence – although an extreme one – of the theoretical framework proposed by Irigaray and taken up by a great many of the difference theorists. Where do we seek this difference between men and women in order to analyse and understand it? Either we find it in the last analysis in the basic bodily difference and therefore return to biological determinism – even if it is enriched and dressed up with psychoanalytical considerations on the processes of the formation of sexual identity. Or difference is socially and historically produced and a result of thousands of years of women's oppression and consequently it is difficult to see it as something to be valued. The risk is that in this infinite research for repressed difference that must be highlighted, we end up idealizing misery. Indeed the female characteristics, which are normally prominently raised by the difference theorists, are dangerously close to the stereotypes created by men and have generally been quite effective in ideologically reinforcing oppression. For example valuing the semiotic order of the mother against the symbolic order of the father, as Kristeva does, leads to conceiving women's exclusion from the spheres of language and concepts as being some fundamental female essence. Conceptual reasoning, language and discourse are the property of the father and men whereas intuition, extra-rational and a-conceptual understanding are the essence of the mother and women. Women having intuition is an old, rather recognizable stereotype. The other side of this coin is the pre-supposition that women are contradictory and not very good at logical thinking. Along the same lines you have the idea that women possess a concrete intelligence of the particular which contrasts with male abstract reasoning. Within left mixed organizations this line of argument supposedly aiming to give value to female difference has only led to theoretical justifications as to why women are continually attributed organizational, rather than political roles. The same positive estimation of hospitality, helpfulness, the absence of aggression and competitiveness that supposedly is enshrined in womenhood leaves out the fact that the counterpart of the absence of aggression and competiveness towards the outside is the violence that women commit in myriad even bizarre ways against themselves. This is not the result of some vocation for maternal caring inscribed indelibly on the female body but of the simple fact hat women have been historically excluded from the use of violence insofar as they have been kept away from the control of its weapons.

As Lidia Cirillo in her book *Lettera alle Romane* [Letter to Roman women] states:

The feminine only exists as a result of an act of power and as an ideology, denying femininity is to refuse to fall into the trap of phallic-logo-centrism, to reject the binary opposition. When a system that denies you is used to affirm you positively then the non-being is turned into its opposite and anti-metaphysical, anti-essentialist and anti-identity intentions are transformed into feminine identity and the metaphysics of sex.

Furthermore, this binary logic removes the possibility of thinking about gender outside of the women/men dichotomy leaving out the experiences and reflections of all those that cannot and do not want to fit into it – gay men, lesbians, transsexuals, bisexuals…

On the contrary, it is on the basis of exactly these experiences that queer theory has developed posing the problem not only of the formation of gender but of its relationship with sex and sexuality. Judith Butler's work probably provides us with the most interesting and intelligent insights on the gender debate in recent years. She has provided us with a number of very interesting and thought-provoking ideas that give her a particular role and position within current feminist debates: the notion of gender performance; the refusal of narrow biological positions or ideas of women's essence; breaking with the women/male dichotomy; the focus on the material aspects of gender oppression (the institutions that reproduce it, the consequences in terms of redistribution, access to welfare, work...); the way in which gender oppression is closely tied up with culture; criticism of heterosexual norms; the refusal of separatism and the attention given to struggles and their framework.

In an article, "Merely Cultural", in which she responds to some of the objections to her ideas made by Nancy Fraser, Butler defines in explicit terms the question of the role played by "obligatory" heterosexuality within capitalist society. Heterosexuality, with its *misrecognition* of homosexuality and other ways of living one's sexuality, is a valid support for the constitution of the mono-nuclear family which plays a central role in the process of reproduction of the labour force and therefore of the overall process of social reproduction of capital as highlighted by Marxist feminists in the 1970s. Imposing the norm of heterosexuality in this way is not a "merely cultural" factor but operates within the economic structure. This is an extremely interesting point and grasps the way in which the role assumed by the family in capitalism is connected to the imposition of obligatory heterosexuality. As Nancy Fraser notes in her response to this article ("Heterosexism, Misrecognition and Capitalism: A response to Judith Butler"), Butler has a certain tendency to confuse what is "material" with what is "economic". Obviously gay, lesbian, transsexual and bisexual oppression has a specifically material aspect because it has consequences and uses means that are definitely material and are not confined to the realm of the "discourse". However another question is whether heterosexism plays a direct role for example in the division of labour and is essential to it, in other words, does it play any role in the structuring of production relations. This theoretical approach, while potentially a very fruitful one, has not yet been taken up by Judith Butler in her writings apart from a few allusions in some articles like "Merely Cultural". Nevertheless it is necessary to theoretically explain how gender performativity operates within capitalist relations of production for a number of reasons. First, we need to avoid an idealist or culturalist approach to how this performativity functions and to steer clear of any ahistorical perspective. What defines a woman as a woman is not invariable and it takes on extremely different connotations through history and the process is not based on the same mechanisms. While gender is continually performed, what is the nature and basis of the coercion of the norm that guarantees the continued repetition of the acts that produce gender performativity and which allows for only two genders to be legitimized? Judith Butler takes up the question of the material nature of how gender is performed and therefore the totality of the material institutions that underpin it which are not reducible to a "language". However dealing with the question only from the point of view of power relations risks obscuring the relations of production which offer the framework for these power relations. Seeing power as only something that is diffuse and everywhere runs the risk of not placing it anywhere, thereby either overestimating the possibility of the autonomous invention of gender or of eliminating it insofar as it is crushed by the unfathomable power relations. Intervening through a "reinvention" within the fissures that are produced in the repetition of the acts that generate gender could be a valid position (also if this is often on paper) by a very limited circle of people equipped with adequate means and with a degree of autonomy that is generally broader than that reserved for mere mortals, but it is not a real option for the rest of humanity. In order to de-construct or re-invent genders therefore you cannot avoid posing the question of which collective subject can do it, able to challenge the material bases which back up coercive heterosexual norms and the woman/man dichotomy. To claim that the subject's gender identity can be constructed through the repetition of performance actions certainly has a grain of truth but risks in time dissipating a subject already suffering from three decades of post-modernism and encourages the idea that it is enough to suspend the repetition in order to escape from a suffocating process of identification. This is certainly not Butler's position – her theoretical solidity prevents her sliding into such naive solutions; but the problem of how to think through the building of collective subjects and the processes becoming subjects – particularly where the subject has undergone the most powerful deconstructions – remains open.

Chapter 4
A QUEER UNION BETWEEN MARXISM AND FEMINISM?

4.1. One theory for dual systems

In 1979, Heidi Hartmann published an essay titled "*The unhappy marriage of Marxism and Feminism*". Lydia Sargent's 1981 anthology, *Women and Revolution: a Discussion of the Unhappy Marriage of Marxism and Feminism,* compiled many of the criticisms and debates surrounding Hartmann's essay, which came from Marxist and radical feminists alike.

In this long article Hartmann develops the so-called dual systems theory, theorizing the intersection of patriarchy and capitalism, starting out from the unsuccessful encounter of Marxism and feminism. Marxism missed the opportunity provided by the new feminist wave to renew itself thoroughly. Instead, it tended to view gender oppression as an oppression of secondary importance and substantially subordinated to class exploitation. The marriage of Marxism and feminism was analogous to marriage of a man and a woman as institutionalized under English common law: like husband and wife, Marxism and feminism were one thing, and that thing was Marxism. Engels' intuition in *The Origin of the Family*, that production and reproduction of immediate life, as a determining factor in history, consisted of two aspects – production of the means of existence and production of human beings themselves – has not been examined in greater depth by Engels himself or by subsequent Marxists. This has contributed to Marxist categories remaining "sex-blind", with consequences not only in terms of underestimating women's condition of oppression, but also undermining the capacity to understand the complex reality of capitalism. Marxist categories such as "class", "reserve army", and "labour force" are "sex-blind" as they are patterned after the "sex-blind" nature of the laws of capitalist development. According to Hartmann, capitalism creates hierarchies within the labour force, but its laws of development cannot determine who will be destined to occupy the different ranks within this hierarchy. From the standpoint of capital's pure "laws of movement", workers occupy a subordinate position whether men or women or white or black, capitalism is utterly indifferent. As long as the categories of the critique of political economy reflect the laws of capitalist development, even these cannot explain who will fit into which rank within the various hierarchies. The concept of class alone is not sufficient in this case and must be integrated with the concepts of gender, race, nationality and religion. In other words, the factor allowing capitalism to confine women to the lower steps of the hierarchy of labour force is not the logic of capitalism's internal functioning itself, but that of another system of oppression. Although this patriarchal system is intertwined with capitalism, it has its own autonomy. Thus the subordination of women created by the patriarchal system, whose origins are pre-capitalist, is used by capitalism for its own purposes.

Hartmann's definition of patriarchy attempts to avoid the pitfall of imagining a universal and invariable structure, rather taking into account its historicity and thus the transformations it has undergone. From this standpoint it is not possible to speak of pure patriarchy, as its material structures are always rooted within determined relations of production and this inextricable relation modifies their characteristics and nature. Instead, one must speak rather of slaveholding patriarchy, feudal patriarchy, capitalist patriarchy and so on. Insisting on the historical nature of patriarchy and its transformation, Hartmann developed an outlook concerning relations between capitalism and patriarchy different from the one Juliet Mitchell put forth in *Psychoanalysis and Feminism*. According to Mitchell, patriarchal structures have a universal and ahistorical psychological and ideological nature, which persists from one mode of production to the next. Interaction between these structures and a given mode of production then produces variations in the way these universal structures are articulated and differentiated. Based on these, female oppression takes different forms and expresses itself in different ways, depending on this historical moment, location and class affiliation.

Instead, Hartmann emphasizes the historical transformations that patriarchal structures themselves, and not just their expressions, undergo. Despite this close correlation between mode of production and patriarchal system, each of these operates according to an internal logic and specific laws that can be on the same wavelength but also in conflict. Despite the fact that capitalism has used and continues to use the patriarchy to shore up its own rule and articulate exploitation, in certain circumstances the "sex-blind" laws movement of capital can come into contradiction with those of the patriarchal system. A failure to grasp the laws proper to the two systems prevents us from understanding the nature of these contradictions. Based on these considerations, the happy marriage Hartmann hopes for should give way to a unified theory able to read and interpret the internal operational laws of the dual capitalist and patriarchal systems and the way in which these relate to one another, without seeking to reduce one to the other.

In the first chapter of her book *Justice Interruptus*, published in 1997, Nancy Fraser developed a theoretical proposal that some critics have also defined as a dual-systems theory. However – as we shall see – Fraser's approach is a rather particular dual-systems theory, very different from Hartmann's outlook. Starting out from the observation that demands for recognition have become almost a paradigmatic form of political conflict at the end of the twentieth century and a fulcrum of struggles relating to nationality, gender, race and sexuality, Fraser proposes a conceptual schema making it possible to take into consideration both the specific differences between demands for justice based on "redistribution" and those based on "recognition" as well as the possibility of linking these. This schema is based on a distinction between injustice with economic roots (exploitation, dispossession, economic marginalization) and injustice of a symbolic and cultural nature (cultural domination, non-recognition, contempt). In analytical terms, disregarding the fact that in reality both forms of oppression are almost always closely intertwined, class exploitation represents a case of "pure" economic injustice, while the oppression of gays and lesbians is a case of cultural injustice: the former case of injustice gives rise to demands for "redistribution"; the latter to demands for "recognition". Asserting that in analytical terms economic and cultural injustice require distinction does not at all equal a failure to recognize their correlation in real life and the circumstance that, for example, the oppression of gays, lesbians, trans and intersexuals exerts leverage on material structures and institutions and has economic consequences and aspects, such as discrimination in the labour market and the healthcare system. But, for example, cultural injustices are not a cornerstone of the relations of production, do not structure the division of labour, and require a symbolic or cultural change to be overcome. Between these two poles, economic injustice and misrecognition, there is a range of injustices that encompass both of these aspects: this is the case of women's and racial oppression. Both have economic roots and are determinant in the division of labour in different ways. In the case of women, this involves both a division of reproductive and productive labour, assigning the former as an unpaid task for women, and a hierarchy within the labour force, where gender is used to distinguish between predominantly male, better-paid job sectors and lower-paid, predominantly female work sectors. However, this is only one aspect of oppression, as women are also subject to depreciation of a symbolic and cultural nature, which gives rise to many forms of discrimination and violence: domestic and sexual violence, sexual exploitation, commodification of women's bodies in communications and information, molestation ...

Thus, oppression of women, like racial oppression, calls for both types of response, namely demands for redistributive justice and for recognition. Fraser does emphasize how this bivalent situation produces contradictions. The logic of demands for redistributive justice, in fact, would lead to doing away with gender or racial distinctions. Calling for economic changes that would entail the end of discrimination on a gender or racial basis in the division of labour, for example, puts the accent on surpassing these identities and differentiation on the basis of these identities. On the other hand, the demand for recognition tends to put a premium on difference and identity, demanding that these be valued positively, instead of as sources of discrimination. How can these two different logics be reconciled? Fraser's response consists in counterposing an "affirmative" approach to a "transformative" one, to the question of redistribution and recognition. Affirmative approaches involve a series of measures in response to economic and social injustices that do not challenge the structure at their roots. This approach would include for example welfare state policies, based on redistributing existing goods to existing groups (for example, social assistance policies in relation to the poor), actually sustaining differentiation between groups. Or multiculturalism, which tends to highlight differences and different identities, demanding respect for these. On the other hand, the transformative approach tends to question the structure generating the injustices, as in the case for socialism in terms of the question of deep transformation of the relations of production and surpassing class divisions, or deconstruction aiming to restructure relations of recognition on a cultural level, playing down or abolishing the differentiations among groups. Queer theory belongs to the latter category. It does not raise the demand for homosexual, trans or intersexual identity as an objective, but rather for the deconstruction of the homosexual/

heterosexual dichotomy, destabilizing all fixed sexual identities. Queer theory seeks to deconstruct gender, as socialism seeks to deconstruct class: neither aim to maintain or affirm gender and class identity – although in political praxis the problem of identity is raised for both – but rather to finally surpass gender, as with class divisions. Based on this common transformative and deconstructionist nature, it is possible to hypothesize a combination of socialism and deconstructionist feminism, able to launch a common attack on economic and cultural injustice alike, offering responses in terms of redistribution and in terms of recognition. This combination is all the more necessary as gender and racial oppression cannot be reduced to either of these forms of injustice, but encompasses both.

4.2. One theory for a single system

Iris Young has criticized both Fraser's theory and Hartman's, in two articles: *"Beyond the Unhappy Marriage: a Critique of the Dual Systems Theory"* and *"Unruly Categories: a Critique of Nancy Fraser's Dual System Theory"*. According to Young, Hartmann's attempt does have the merit of providing an alternative to an ahistorical concept of the patriarchy, but raises other problems. Of course, the oppression of women goes back much further than the advent of capitalism, so its cause cannot be found within the capitalist mode of production. However, the same discourse is applicable to class divisions and exploitation: they are not an original invention of capitalism and indeed also constituted the basis of the functioning of the economy within slaveholding and feudal modes of production. We must deduct from this that class division and exploitation represent a freestanding structure changing historically with the succession of modes of production, but nevertheless maintaining autonomy from the mode of production itself. In this sense could class division constitute a system apart form capitalism, but intertwined with it afterwards? Accepting the fact that there is no "pure" division into classes, separate from a specific mode of production determining it, generally leads to the idea that class division in itself does not constitute a system that endures while changing over the course of centuries. Why would the same not apply also to patriarchy? Moreover, the dual systems theory enables traditional Marxism to continue to build its theory of production relations and social changes and analyse capitalism in an unchanged way, applying "sex-blind" categories, and to leave the task of analysing the patriarchal system up to feminism. Against this option, Young proposes instead to integrate Marxism by developing a theory of gender division of labour, referring to all differentiations of labour by gender within society, from reproductive labour within the family to gender hierarchy within the labour force in the productive sphere.

One of the reasons motivating Young's critique of Hartmann, and that recurs in the case of the critique of Fraser's dual systems theory, is the refusal to assign only the categories of the critique of political economy to Marxism, and not those pertaining to cultural criticism. Making Marxism coincide with the economic analysis of capitalism, actually makes it a reductive concept. In the same way, it is an error to counterpose the economic and cultural spheres as if they were two completely autonomous spheres that come to interact in a reciprocal relationship. And yet we must say, contrary to Young's critique, Fraser's writing was and remains guided by a diametrically opposite objective, surpassing the separation between the cultural and economic spheres and building a theoretical framework capable of highlighting how they intertwine. From this standpoint, it is difficult to consider her position as a version of the dual systems theory, or if so, it is an utterly specific version. According to Young, when one moves from an abstractly analytical environment to examining how oppressions and exploitation and the dynamics of different struggles function concretely, one can see how a binary opposition between redistribution and recognition does not fully express the complexity of the processes of developing subjectivities that spur on the community or groups to struggle. The logic of demands for recognition does not necessarily contradict the logic of demands for redistribution, to the extent that they both contribute to building identities able to struggle for economic justice and social equality: this is the case with Zapatism and Black Power. As long as the cultural oppression of specific groups plays a part in their economic oppression, the two struggles are not in conflict, but rather contiguous. According to Young, the politics of affirming identity (of race, gender, ethnic group or religion), comes into contradiction with the struggle for social justice only where instead of contributing to the process of subjectivization, it puts the cultural expression to the fore as an end in itself, so as to overshadow the role of culture in the production of structural economic oppressions.

The discussion on the dual systems' credibility or lack thereof is also present to some extent, embedded in another debate that took place in the 1980s among Marxist and socialist feminists in the pages of two journals, *New Left Review* and *Studies in Political Economy*. Central to the debate in which authors such as Johanna Brenner, Maria Ramas, Michèle Barrett, and Patricia Connelly participated, was whether or not it is possible to combine Marxism and feminism, to develop a Marxist feminist theory, confronting the various problems raised by such an attempt. Although all the participants in this debate tended to negate the validity of a dual systems theory, while recognizing that women's oppression precedes capitalism, they had different ways of seeking to show how and in what sense this oppression links up with capitalism. Many questions were raised: are there patriarchal structures independent of capitalism's own? What role does ideology play in gender oppression? What relation is there between gender ideology and the material bases of women's oppression? Does the material and economic oppression of women also produce patriarchal ideology or on the contrary, does the latter also exert an influence on the economic level, for example on the sexual division of labour?

In *Women's Oppression Today*, Michèle Barrett sought to show the role played by ideology in constructing the economy, emphasizing how many of the categories we refer to as economic have been constructed historically in ideological terms. In the same way, the reasons for which the ideology of the typically bourgeois family has been and continues to be shared, even by the working class, warrant investigation. Barrett's attempt proceeds from the consideration that it is not possible to oppose women's economic situation and ideology, since such a distinction does not make it possible to grasp how these facets are intertwined. On the contrary, it is necessary to explore the complex dynamics of how gender and class ideology relate to one another. Brenner and Ramas criticized Michèle Barrett's essay in an article published in *New Left Review*, as did Pat and Hugh Armstrong in the pages of *Studies in Political Economy*. According to her critics, Michèle Barrett had fallen back into the dual systems theory trap, while on the contrary it is necessary to recognize that, despite the fact that the patriarchy did not originate with capitalism, but preceded it, it has become completely integrated by capitalism to the extent that by now they act together, not constituting two systems, but a same and single system. In support of this position, Brenner and Ramas insisted on the role biology plays in the sexual division of labour that took place in the course of nineteenth-century capitalist development. Women's reproductive role, the lack of effective contraception, and lack of alternatives to breastfeeding came into contradiction with full participation in productive factory work. As breastfeeding and childrearing were incompatible with factory work, this combination of a biological factor and a specific type of economic development produced the specific oppression of women under capitalism, based on the family home system. The crux of the matter consisted in how the capitalist class productive system incorporated biological reproductive facts and how biological differences in this specific situation became an obstacle to women's participation in production. Insisting on the weight of the biological factor viewed in relation to the social factor and the historical modifications of this relation is tantamount to downplaying the role of patriarchal ideology in the determination of the sexual division of labour.

In her response to this criticism (*Rethinking Women's*

Oppression: A Reply to Brenner and Ramas), Michèle Barrett noted that the responses given to biological limits are always *social.* Women of the aristocracy and the grand bourgeoisie were quick to resolve the need to feed newborns through the use of wet-nurses. Moreover, in some societies, the problem of breastfeeding is partially socialized so as to relieve the burden falling upon the mother alone. For working-class women in countries undergoing capitalist development, the response has been to marginalize women from productive work. In other terms, the type of response given to a biological limitation (for example the need to breastfeed babies) is a question of social choices and processes. But these choices and processes can only be understood by taking into account gender ideology and how it influences and has influenced the division of labour.

4.3. From unhappy marriage to queer union

The various versions of feminist theory have often, if not always, been attempts to provide answers to the major problems facing women on the political level, and in particular those pertaining to constructing a female and/or feminist subjectivity able to struggle for women's own liberation. Questions such as valuing or deconstructing gender difference, the social or biological origin of the oppression of women, to what extent there is a current patriarchal system autonomous from capitalism, the role of gender ideology with respect to the sexual division of labour, or whether or not sexual classes exist, are the reflection of concrete political challenges to which the feminist movement has had to attempt to provide answers. These responses, in turn, have had a decisive influence on the movement's development, its fragmentation and its articulation.

The brief reconstruction of some of these debates provided in these pages has attempted to follow a logic and classifications not generally used in the feminist debate, seeking instead to attempt to circle round an unresolved political problem that is nevertheless all the more urgent; namely, the historical, political and theoretical relationship between gender and class and the possibility of developing a theory that reconciles Marxism and feminism without forcing them into a marriage of convenience. Addressing this problem has become all the more urgent if we consider the developments in the feminist movement in recent decades and the impact of capitalist globalization on women's lives.

Faced with the monumental process of feminization of labour underway, produced by capitalist globalization, the substantial divorce between Marxism and feminism has given rise to still more major problems. On the one hand, analysis of the sexual division of labour, of the role of reproduction for capitalism, and the way patriarchal ideology is interwoven with the dynamics of capitalist accumulation, continues to not be fully integrated either in Marxist theory or in the actions of organizations of the political left and social movements. This greatly limits both understanding and the capacity to intervene in reality. On the other, the fact that a consistent part of feminist movements and theory disregards class determinations in the name of a universal sisterhood or qualities that are essential female characteristics makes it more difficult to build political and social alliances between the feminist movement and the workers' movement and does not even render a good service to the feminist movement itself and its capacity to transform reality.

As early as the end of the 1980s, the theory of intersectionality (a term coined in 1989 by Kimberlé Crenshaw) has attempted to put the emphasis on the interaction between gender, class and race and on how this complex interaction acted in turn on subjects. This interaction must not be understood as a simple addition or summing up of oppressions.

Due to this very intersection, women cannot be viewed as a homogenous subject experiencing gender oppression as primary and sexism as their main relation to power, given their diversity in racial, class, ethnic and status terms and how this diversification and interaction of elements play a part in forming their subjectivity.

The question of the relationship between capitalism and

patriarchy must be examined just as thoroughly. Contrary to theories that attempt to conceive of the relationship between men and women in terms of exploitation; as a form of organization of a sector of production patriarchy has long ceased its function: what remained of it has been overtaken by capitalism. The process has been anything but linear. On the one hand, capitalism has broken the economic ties based on patriarchy, on the other, however, it has conserved and used patriarchal power relations and ideology in many ways. It has broken up the family as a productive unit, but it has used the latter and transformed it profoundly to ensure that the task of reproducing the labour force for it gets done. Here patriarchal power relations have played their part: capitalism needed to offload reproductive tasks onto the family – and subordination of women guaranteed the outcome – aggravating the burden on women and the oppressive relations between men and women.

Recognizing that in this context men, including working-class men, enjoyed and continue to enjoy a relative benefit from gender oppression does not mean viewing men as an exploiter class, but understanding the complexity with which capitalism integrates and employs pre-capitalist power relations to create hierarchies of exploited and oppressed, digging trenches and raising barriers. The same applies to the relationship between women and work, a question that has become central with the continual growth in female employment and which also raises the need for deepening the theory of the sexual division of labour that does not concentrate only or above all on reproductive labour. Race and gender have been and continue to be powerful instruments in the division of labour. "Feminization of labour" has a dual meaning at the very least. That women take an ever-greater part in productive labour, is a fact that cannot help but modify their condition and the forms that oppression takes. But also the use of a female labour force plays an essential role from capital's standpoint as it has done in the past: it is used to deskill productive sectors and lower labour costs, to worsen working conditions and implement casualization of work.

Once again, understanding this dynamic is impossible without reference to the fundamental role of patriarchal ideology and patriarchal power relations. This is a role that not only moves towards an implicit or explicit devaluation of female labour, invariably viewed as secondary, as an adjunct to male labour, but which has effects and creates problems also in terms of class subjectivity, often making it more difficult for women to mobilize and speak out. Underevaluating or not dealing with the interweave of economic conditions and cultural and ideological oppressions entails the risk of losing sight of the complexity the task of building a new workers' movement of men and women alike will increasingly confront, faced with an ever more female working class.

Feminism has developed tools essential to the understanding of gender reality, how it functions and its mechanisms. In its contradictory relationship with psychoanalysis, it has nevertheless shed light on the psychological component of women's oppression and on the role of the family and family relations as an essential locus for reproducing the sexual division of roles, of the construction of gender and the consolidation and perpetuation of normative heterosexuality. Fully assuming these aspects does not necessarily mean abandoning a materialist approach to go back to the "clouds of idealism". Rather, it means grasping the way patriarchal power is internalized, even by women themselves, acting on a level that is not economic, and as such this internalization also has decisive effects from a political standpoint. Anyone who has an experience of political activism has seen up close the problems women have speaking out, voicing their initiative, becoming politicized, as they are crushed between interiorized gender oppression and the doubt in one's abilities this entails and how oppression mechanisms come into play in power relations with male members of their organizations. Disregarding these elements not only does a disservice to women, it also does a disservice to Marxism and to a political project aimed at radical transformation of society.

Developing an outlook that can make sense of intersections

and decipher the complex relationship between patriarchal holdovers that drift like homeless ghosts in the globalized capitalist world and patriarchal structures that, on the contrary, have been integrated, used and transformed by capitalism calls for a renewal of Marxism. This renewal is necessary in order to go beyond counterposing cultural and economic, material and ideological categories. A political project aiming to rebuild a new workers' movement requires serious reflection on how gender and race influence both the composition of the labour force and the processes of developing subjectivity. Moreover, it also means an end to the contest over primary oppression. The point is not whether class comes before gender or gender before class, the point is rather how gender and class intertwine in capitalist production and power relations to give rise to a complex reality, and it makes little sense and is not very useful to attempt to reduce these to a simple formula. The point is, therefore how class and gender can be combined together in a political project able to take action avoiding two specular dangers: the temptation of mashing the two realities together, making gender a class or class a gender, and the temptation to pulverize power relations and exploitative relations to see nothing but a series of single oppressions lined up beside each other and reluctant to be included within a comprehensive liberation project.

People mentioned in the text

Inessa Armand (1874–1920) was a French revolutionary and feminist who moved to Moscow at the age of five and was politically active there in the Social Democratic Labour Party. She was involved in organizing women including by organizing the anti-war International Conference of Socialist Women in Switzerland in 1915, chairing the first International Conference of Communist Women in 1920 and being the director of Zhenotdel, the Communist women's organization in the Soviet Union after the Russian Revolution.

Pat and Hugh Armstrong are respectively Director of the School of Canadian Studies, and a teacher in the School of Social Work, at Carleton University in Ottawa. They have written extensively together on questions of health care and on women's segregation in the workforce.

Johann Jakob Bachofen (1815–1887) was a Swiss anthropologist whose seminal 1861 book *Mother Rite* influenced many others including Engels.

Michèle Barrett is Professor of Modern Literary and Cultural Theory at Queen Mary University London. Her best-known contribution to feminist thinking is *Women's Oppression Today: Problems in Marxist-Feminist Analysis* (1980, revised edition 1988).

Frances Beal is a black feminist and a peace and justice activist. In 1968, she co-founded the Black Women's Liberation Committee of the Student Nonviolent Coordinating Committee (SNCC). In 1969 she wrote *Double Jeopardy: To Be Black & Female.*

Simone de Beauvoir (1908–1986) was a French writer, philosopher, feminist and social theorist. Her book *The Second Sex*, published in 1949, was groundbreaking but she is also well known for her novels, especially *She Came to Stay* (1943, English 1949) and *The Mandarins* (1954, English 1956).

Daniel Bensaïd (1946–2010) was one of France's most prominent Marxist philosophers and wrote extensively on that and other subjects. Only one major work has been published in English, *Marx for Our Times: Adventures and Misadventures of a Critique* (2002). He was for many years a leading member of the Ligue Communiste Revolutionaire (LCR, Revolutionary Communist League) the French section of the Fourth International and subsequently of the Noveau Parti Anticapitaliste (NPA, New Anticapitalist Party).

August Bebel (1840–1913) was a German Marxist, orator and writer and one of the founders of the Sozialdemokratische Partei Deutschlands (SPD) the German Social Democratic Party. His book *Women under Socialism* (1879, English 1910) was both influential and controversial.

Enrico Berlinger (1922–1984) was National Secretary of the Partito Comunista Italiano (PCI, Italian Communist Party) from 1972 until his death. He was a prominent leader of the Eurocommunist current.

Johanna Brenner is an American socialist feminist and sociologist. She is Emeritus Professor of Women's Studies at Portland State University. She is a member of the Advisory Board of the US socialist magazine *Against the Current.* Her book *Women and the Politics of Class* was published in 2000.

Judith Butler is an American post-structuralist philosopher who has written extensively in the fields of feminist and queer theory, political philosophy and ethics. She is a professor in the Rhetoric and Comparative Literature departments at the University of California, Berkeley. Two of her most important works are *Gender Trouble* (1990) and *Bodies that Matter* (1993).

Stokely Carmichael (1941–1998) was a black American activist; a leader of the Student Nonviolent Coordinating Committee (SNCC) who went on to lead the Black Panthers. He popularized the term Black Power and is (in)famous for the, possibly ironic, statement that "the position of women in the movement is prone".

Adriana Caverero is an Italian feminist and philosopher. She is Professor of Political Philosophy at the University of Verona. Her work *Per una teoria della differenza sessuale* (1987) [For a theory of sexual difference] has been particularly influential in terms of feminist thinking.

Lidia Cirillo is a feminist activist and a prominent figure in the World March of Women in Italy. She has also been a leading member of the Fourth Internationalist current in Italy since the 1960s. She is the founder of the *Quaderni Viola* (Purple notebooks, a feminist review) and author of several feminist works: *Meglio Orfane* (1992) (Better to be Orphans), *Lettera alle Romane* (Letter to Roman Women) (2001), and most recently *La Luna Severa Maestra* (The Moon, a Strict Mistress) (2003) on the relationship between feminism and social movements.

Hélène Cixous is a French feminist writer, poet, playwright, philosopher and literary critic. She is professor at Cornell University. Together with Luce Irigaray and Julia Kristeva she is one of the most prominent representatives of differentialist feminist theory. She has also written widely on James Joyce and on Jacques Derrida.

Stephanie Coontz is a feminist writer and historian. She teaches history and family studies at The Evergreen State College, Olympia Washington. She has written extensively on the history of the family. Her most recent books are *"A Strange Stirring": The Feminine Mystique and American Women at the Dawn of the 1960s* (2011) and *Marriage, A History: How Love Conquered Marriage* (2005).

Kimberlé Crenshaw is a professor at the UCLA School of Law and Columbia Law School specializing in race and gender issues. She is a leading proponent of Critical Race Theory (CRT). She was also the first person to use the term intersectionality which has become has become a key tool in understanding the interplay and interaction between class, race and gender (and other oppressions beyond these).

Mariarosa Dalla Costa is an Italian feminist and professor of political science at the University of Padua. She wrote a pamphlet *The Power of Women and the Subversion of the Community* with Selma James in 1972. This became the founding text of the "wages for housework" current.

Heather Dashner is a longstanding feminist and political activist in Mexico. She is the author of "Feminism to the tune of the cumbia..." published in Spanish as a pamphlet by the PRT Mexico (1987) and co-editor with Penelope Duggan of the IIRE Notebook *Women's Lives in the New Global Economy* (1992).

Angela Davis is an American thinker, scholar and activist working on feminism, African American studies and opposition to the US prison system among other topics. She was a member of the Communist Party USA, a leader of the Civil Rights Movement, and a sympathizer of the Black Panther Party. Among her books is *Women, Race, & Class* (1983). Together with Kimberlé Crenshaw and others, she formed the African American Agenda 2000, an alliance of Black feminists.

Olympe de Gouges (1748-1793) drew up the most comprehensive manifesto of bourgeois feminism during the French revolution: *The Declaration of the Rights of Women and Female Citizens* (1791).

Christine Delphy is a French feminist writer and theorist. She was a founder with Simone de Beauvoir of *Nouvelles questions féministes* [New feminist questions] in 1977. She is one of the most prominent thinkers of materialist feminism. Her essay "L'ennemi principal" [The Main Enemy] (1970) had a powerful impact.

Jeanne Deroin (1805–1894) was an editorial board member of *Voix des Femmes* (Women's Voice), a founder of another newspaper, *L'Opinion des femmes* (Women's Opinion), she was heavily involved in the feminist movement and actively supported workers in the 1848 French Revolution. She dedicated herself to building an association of workers' organizations based on parity of rights for women and men and wrote the programmatic documents for this association. She was arrested on 29 May 1850 and accused of conspiracy, but she was pressured by her comrades not to reveal her role in the association for fear that it would be generally discredited if it became known. In the end she caved in.

Elizabeth Dmitrieff (1851–1910 or 1918) was a Russian-born feminist and active participant the 1871 Paris Commune, notably as a co-founder of the "Women's Union for the Defence of Paris and Aid to the Wounded" (Union des Femmes pour la défense de Paris et les soins aux blessés), created on 11 April 1871. She was active in her youth in the socialist circles of Saint Petersburg. In 1868, she travelled to Switzerland, and co-founded the Russian section of the First International. She met Marx in London, who sent her in March 1871, to cover the events of the Commune. She contributed to the socialist newspaper *La Cause du peuple*. After having fought on the barricades during the Bloody Week, she fled to Russia, where she died in Siberia accompanying her husband in deportation.

Andrea Dworkin (1946–2005) was an American radical feminist and writer best known for her criticism of pornography, which she argued was linked to rape and violence against women more generally. An anti-war activist and anarchist in the late 1960s, Dworkin wrote 10 books on radical feminist theory and practice. Her two best-known books are probably *Pornography: Men Possessing Women* (1979) and *Intercourse* (1987).

Friedrich Engels (1820–1895) was a philosopher and economist. Life-long collaborator of Karl Marx with whom he published *The Communist Manifesto* in 1848. Among his most significant works were *Conditions of the Working Class in England* (1844) and *The Origin of the Family, Private Property and the State* (1884).

Shulamith Firestone (1945–2012) was a Canadian-born feminist. She was a central figure in the early development of radical feminism, having been a founding member of the New

York Radical Women, Redstockings, and New York Radical Feminists. In 1970, she authored *The Dialectic of Sex: The Case for Feminist Revolution*, an important and widely influential feminist work.

Michel Foucault (1926–1984) was a French philosopher, social theorist, historian of ideas, and literary critic who initially embraced and then distanced himself from structuralism. His writing especially his three-volume *History of Sexuality* (1976-1984, English 1977, 1985, 1986) had an important impact on a number of feminist writers.

Antoinette Fouque was the leader of the Psychoanalysis and Politics (known as Psych et Po) tendency within the French women's liberation movement (MLF). This current provoked a sharp polemic when it tried to register the MLF name as its property, leading to a definitive split with the rest of the movement. It has a publishing house, "éditions des femmes".

Charles Fourier (1772–1837) was a French philosopher. His *Theory of Four Movements* (1808, English 1996) in particular had an important impact on socialist feminist thinking of the time. He is credited with being the first person to use the word "feminism".

Nancy Fraser is an American critical theorist, currently the Henry A. and Louise Loeb Professor of Political and Social Science and professor of philosophy at The New School for Social Research in New York. She has written extensively on feminism including in *Justice Interruptus: Critical Reflections on the "Postsocialist" Condition* (1997)

Sigmund Freud (1856–1939) was an Austrian neurologist who became known as the founding father of psychoanalysis. There has been a great deal of debate about the extent to which some of his theories were based on and perpetuate patriarchal assumptions (see also Juliet Mitchell).

Betty Friedan (1921–2006) was an American feminist writer and activist. Her 1963 book *The Feminine Mystique* is often credited with sparking the "second wave" of American feminism. In 1966, Friedan founded and was elected the first president of the National Organization for Women.

Heidi Hartmann is a feminist economist and research professor and founder of the Institute for Women's Policy Research at the George Washington University. She is the author of the essay "The Unhappy Marriage of Marxism and Feminism" (1979) in *Capital and Class*.

Casey Hayden was a leading activist in the Civil Rights movement during the 1960s. She was a founding member of Students for a Democratic Society (SDS) and worked as a volunteer for the Student Nonviolent Coordinating Committee (SNCC). With Mary King she wrote the "SNCC Position Paper: Women in the Movement" (1964) which criticized the gendered division of labour within the movement.

Henrik Ibsen (1828–1906) was a major 19th-century Norwegian playwright, theatre director, and poet. He is often referred to as "the father of realism" and is one of the founders of Modernism in the theatre. Two of his major plays *The Doll's House* (1879) and *Hedda Gabbler* (1890) have central female protagonists.

Luce Irigaray is a Belgian feminist, philosopher, linguist, psychoanalyst, sociologist and cultural theorist. She is best known for her works *Speculum of the Other Woman* (1974) and *This Sex Which Is Not One* (1977) and *Temps de la Différence* [Time of difference] (1989).

Selma James is an American-born feminist based in Britain. Her pamphlet *The Power of Women and the Subversion of the Community*, written with Mariarosa Dalla Costa in 1972, was the founding text of the "wages for housework" current. She has a long history of activism on questions of anti-racism, anti-colonialism and feminism. Currently she is coordinator of the Global Women's Strike.

Jane Kelly is a British socialist feminist and a leading member of Socialist Resistance. She taught women's studies and art history at Kingston University and has written on many feminist issues, including "Postmodernism and Feminism: The Road to Nowhere" in Dave Hill, Pete McLaren, Mike Cole and Glen Rikowski (eds) *Postmodernism in Educational Theory: Education and the Politics of Human Resistance*, (1999) "Unfinished Business: Women still unequal after 40 years" in Mike Cole (ed) *Education, Equality and Human Rights: Issues of gender, 'race', sexuality, disability and social class*, (2012).

Mary King was an activist in the Student Nonviolent Coordinating Committee (SNCC) in the United States in the 1960s. With Casey Hayden she wrote the "SNCC Position Paper: Women in the Movement" (1964) which criticized the gendered division of labour within the movement.

Anne Koedt is a United States radical feminist and NY based author of *The Myth of the Vaginal Orgasm*, 1970, the classic feminist work on women's sexuality. She was connected to the group New York Radical Women and was a founding member in 1969 of New York Radical Feminists in the group's first consciousness-raising and organizing group, The Stanton-Anthony Brigade, with Shulamith Firestone and others.

Alexandra Kollontai (1872–1952) was a Russian Bolshevik who worked to organize women in support of the revolutionary cause. She was also a writer both of political propaganda often aimed at women and taking up questions of sexual and emotional relationships amongst other things. She also wrote novels including *The Love of Worker Bees* (English 1978). In 1919 she became one of the first female government ministers in Europe. In 1923, she was appointed Soviet Ambassador to Norway, becoming the world's first female ambassador in modern times.

Julia Kristeva is a philosopher, psychoanalyst, feminist, and critical theorist. Born in Bulgaria she has lived in France since the mid-1960s. She is now a Professor at the University of Paris

Diderot. Her first book *Séméiôtiké*, published in 1969 was very influential.

Nadezhda Krupskaya (1869–1939) was a Russian Bolshevik revolutionary and politician. She married the Russian revolutionary leader Vladimir Lenin in 1898. She was deputy minister (Commissar) of Education in 1929–1939. She supported but was not directly involved in the specific organization of women.

Jacques Lacan (1901–1981) was a French psychoanalyst and psychiatrist who made prominent contributions to psychoanalysis and philosophy, and has been called "the most controversial psychoanalyst since Freud". Lacan's post-structuralist theory rejected the belief that reality can be captured in language. His concept "the mirror stage" (*stade du miroir*) in particular has been analysed by Luce Irigaray.

Ferdinand Lassalle (1825–1864) was a German philosopher, and socialist political activist. Lassalle and his supporters proposed to ban women working in industry. In general he was hostile to the ideas of Marx and Engels and vice versa.

Eleanor Burke Leacock (1922–1987) was an American theorist of anthropology working from a Marxist perspective who focused particularly on the question of gender. One of her most important contributions was her essay "Interpreting the Origins of Gender Inequality: Conceptual and Historical Problems" (1983). She was also the editor of versions of Henry Morgan's *Ancient Society* and Friedrich Engels' *The Origin of the Family, Private Property and the State*.

Vladimir Lenin (1870–1924) was a Russian revolutionary, politician and political theorist and leader of the Russian revolution. Lenin was supportive of the efforts to organize women as a specific part of the movement.

Claude Lévi-Strauss (1908–2009) was a highly influential French anthropologist and ethnologist. His work especially *Structural Anthropology* (1958, English 1963) and *Elementary*

Kinship Structures (1949, English 1969) had an important influence on second wave feminism especially on Simone de Beauvoir.

Carla Lonzi (1931–1982) was an Italian writer and art critic and feminist theoretician of sexual difference, founder of the feminist group Rivolta femminile (Female Revolt) in the 1970s. Her *Sputiamo su Hegel* (We Spit on Hegel) (1974) was the founding text of this wave of Italian feminism.

Rosa Luxemburg (1871–1919) was a Marxist theorist, philosopher, economist and revolutionary socialist of Polish descent who became a naturalized German citizen and played a major role in the left wing of the socialist movement in Germany. She engaged in major debates with Lenin on the national question. Although she was not involved either in her practice or her writing in specifically studying women's oppression it was obviously inspiring to have such a strong woman leader, alongside her close friend Clara Zetkin (see below). She opposed any attempt by social democratic parties to abandon the demand for womens right to vote insisting they must stand firm for true universal suffrage. In 1919, after the crushing of the Spartacus League uprising, Luxemburg and other leaders were captured and murdered.

Mary Macarthur (1880–1921) was a trade unionist and women's rights campaigner. She was the Secretary of the Women's Trade Union League. In 1906 she founded the National Federation of Women Workers, a general labour union, "open to all women in unorganized trades or who were not admitted to their appropriate trade union". In 1910 she led women chainmakers in a successful 10-week strike for higher pay in the West Midlands.

Catharine MacKinnon is an American feminist scholar and activist who has written particularly on the question of pornography, for example *Pornography and Civil Rights: A New Day for Women's Equality* (1988). She is professor of law at the University of Michigan Law School.

Eleanor Marx (1855–1898) was the youngest daughter of Karl Marx and herself a political activist. In 1884, she joined the Social Democratic Federation (SDF) led by Henry Hyndman and was elected to its executive but then left and founded the Socialist League, mainly on account of Hyndman's nationalism. She became involved in the Women's Trade Union League and went on to support numerous strikes. She also helped organize the Gasworkers' Union. She wrote many articles and pamphlets including *The Woman Question* (1886).

Karl Marx (1818–1883) was a German philosopher, economist and revolutionary socialist. His ideas played a significant role in the development of the socialist movement. He published various books during his lifetime, with the most notable being *The Communist Manifesto* (1848) and *Capital* (1867–1894). His 1844 *Economic and Philosophical Manuscripts* saw the position of women as a barometer for the level of overall development of a society.

Louise Michel (1830–1905) was an anarchist and activist in the Paris Commune, participating as an ambulance woman and in the last stand in Bloody Week. She was imprisoned for 20 months and then deported to New Caledonia for 7 years – only being allowed to return to France when the Communards were pardoned in 1880. She published her Memoirs in 1886.

Kate Millet is an American feminist writer and activist. She is best known for her 1970 book, *Sexual Politics* but has also written a number of novels including *Flying* (1974) and *Sita* (1977).

Juliet Mitchell is a British psychoanalyst and socialist feminist. Her first book *Woman's Estate* (1971) based on her 1966 article for the influential British *New Left Review* was relatively significant at the time but it is for her next *Psychoanalysis and Feminism* (1974) for which she is best known. While mounting a sharp critique of aspects of Freud's theories she never the less defended the practice of psychoanalysis.

Rita Montagnana (1895–1979) was a founder of the Italian Communist Party and attended the Third Congress of the Comintern in 1921 on behalf of the PCI. She was a founder of the Union of Italian Women (UDI), a PCI front organization, and director of its newspaper *Noi Donne* (We Women). Her books include *La famiglia, il divorzio, l'amore nel pensiero delle donne comuniste* (The family, divorce, love the thought of Communist women) (1945).

Henry Morgan (1818–1881) was a pioneering American anthropologist and social theorist, a railroad lawyer and capitalist. His best-known book *Ancient Society (1877)*, had a major impact on his contemporaries Marx and Engels and is cited by Engels in *Origin of the Family, Private Property and the State*.

Robin Morgan is an American poet, author, political theorist and activist, journalist, lecturer, and former child actor. Since the early 1960s she has been a key radical feminist. Her 1970 anthology *Sisterhood Is Powerful* is her best-known work.

Luisa Muraro is an Italian philosopher and writer and one of the first Italian feminists to take up and develop the "difference theory" originally put forward by Irigaray and Kristeva. Her books include *L'ordine simbolico della madre* (The mother's symbolic order), 2006.

Christabel Pankhurst (1880–1958) was a suffragette born in Manchester, England. Together with her mother Emmeline, she founded the Women's Social and Political Union (WSPU) and ran the organization during her mother's frequent periods of imprisonment. She also directed its militant actions from exile in France from 1912 to 1913. She took the same position as her mother at the outbreak of the 1914 war. After the war she moved to the United States and became an evangelist.

Emmeline Pankhurst (1858–1928) was a British suffragette. She founded the Women's Social and Political Union (WSPU) in 1898 an organization committed to militant tactics such as the smashing of windows and later arson to win women's suffrage. She was sent to prison on a number of occasions. After the outbreak of the First World War in 1914, Emmeline together with her eldest daughter Christabel supported the government and called for halt to militant action. She opposed the Russian Revolution and in later life joined the Conservative Party.

Sylvia Pankhurst (1882–1960) was involved along with her mother Emmeline and sister Christabel in the suffrage movement and the WSPU in particular. However she concentrated on building the WPSU in the East End of London amongst working-class women. Political disagreements with her mother and sister came to a head when they supported the war in 1914. Sylvia broke with the WSPU at this point and founded the East London Federation of Suffragettes (ELFS), which later evolved politically and changed its name, first to Women's Suffrage Federation and then to the Workers' Socialist Federation. The WSF was involved in the founding of the Communist Party in Britain though the association did not last. Sylvia by this time defined herself as a left Communist and had some strong disagreements with Lenin. Later she devoted more of her energy to anti-fascism and anti-colonialism and became a strong supporter of Ethiopia and Haile Selassie.

Pier Paolo Pasolini (1922– 975) was an Italian film director, poet, writer and intellectual. He was a fellow traveller of the Italian Communist Party for some time and joined in 1947. He was openly gay from the beginning of his career. In 1949 he was charged with the corruption of minors and obscene acts in public places and expelled from the Communist Party. Later he cooperated with Lotta Continua.

Emma Patterson (1848–1886) was an English feminist and trade unionist. In 1875 Patterson founded the Women's Protective and Provident League, which became the Women's Trade Union League in 1903. As well as supporting demands common to all trade unions they also campaigned for maternity leave, co-operative homes for working women and votes for all women – not just the property owners.

Pierre-Joseph Proudhon (1809–1865) was a French economist and philosopher. He was the first person to call himself an anarchist and also coined the phrase "property is theft". As well as his conservative ideas on the question of women's role he is also alleged to have made anti-semitic remarks.

Alisa Del Re is associate professor at the Faculty of Political Science at the University of Padua. She is director of the Interdepartmental Research Centre: Studies on Gender Politics and a member of the steering committee of the international review *Cahiers du Genre.*

Ermanno Rea is an Italian journalist and writer. His disturbing autobiographical novel Mistero napoletano (Neapolitan Mystery – 1986) was well acclaimed and won a literary prize as did his two subsequent novels.

Shelia Rowbotham is a British socialist feminist theorist and writer from a libertarian perspective. Her books include *Women, Resistance and Revolution* (1972), *Hidden from History* (1974), *Women's Consciousness, Men's World* (1973) and *Beyond the Fragments: Feminism and the Making of Socialism* (1980) (co-authored with Lynne Segal and Hilary Wainwright).

Gayle S. Rubin is a cultural anthropologist, an activist and theorist of sex and gender politics. She is an Associate Professor of Anthropology and Women's Studies at University of Michigan at Ann Arbor. She first came to prominence in 1975 with her essay "The Traffic in Women: Notes on the 'Political Economy' of Sex".

Ferdinand de Saussure (1857–1913) was a Swiss linguist who is considered one of the founders of 20th century linguistics and of semiotics. His most influential work, *Course in General Linguistics* (Cours de linguistique générale), was published posthumously in 1916.

Henri Saint Simon (1760–1825) was a French utopian socialist, a supporter of the American Revolution and of the French revolution of 1789. He was imprisoned during the Terror for suspected counter-revolutionary activities. His key ideas were about administrative efficiency and industrialism, and a belief that science was the key to progress. While he had few supporters in his lifetime, after his death his ideas became more popular and the movement known as Saint-Simonianism was important in the first half of the 19th century in France.

Lydia Sargent is an American feminist. Her 1981 anthology, *Women and Revolution: a Discussion of the Unhappy Marriage of Marxism and Feminism* reprinted Heidi Hartmann's "The Unhappy Marriage of Marxism and Feminism". Together with Michael Albert and a number of others she founded South End Press in 1977 as well as *Z Magazine* ("independent magazine of critical thinking on political, cultural, social, and economic life in the US"), which she co-edits and co-produces.

Lynne Segal is an Australian-born, British-based socialist feminist. She is Professor of Psychology and Gender Studies at Birkbeck, University of London. Her early influential works include *Is the Future Female? Troubled Thoughts on Contemporary Feminism* (1987) and *Beyond the Fragments* (with Sheila Rowbotham and Hilary Wainwright, 1980).

Yakov Sverdlov (1885–1919) was a leader of the Bolshevik Party and President of the Russian Soviet Republic. He was a close ally of Lenin.

William Thompson (1775–1833) was an Irish political writer and thinker. His ideas influenced the Cooperative movement, the Chartists and Karl Marx. He developed a critique of the contemporary status of women, was hostile to Malthus and was a supporter of contraception. His works include *Appeal of One Half the Human Race, Women, Against the Pretensions of the Other Half, Men, to Retain Them in Political, and thence in Civil and Domestic Slavery* (1825).

Flora Tristan (1803–1844) was a French socialist writer and activist and one of the founders of modern feminism. Her best-known writings are *Peregrinations of a Pariah* (1838),

Promenades in London (1840), and *The Workers' Union* (1843). She wrote this latter after an extensive stay in Peru and a short trip to Britain, where she produced works on the social conditions along the Channel.

Leon Trotsky (1879–1940) was a revolutionary Marxist and leader of the Russian Revolution. He was leader of the Left Opposition in the 1920s after Stalin's rise in the Soviet Union. Exiled from Russia he continued his political work abroad until he was assassinated in Mexico in 1940 by a Stalinist agent. He wrote a number of articles on the situation of women in the Soviet Union, and in his book *The Revolution Betrayed* argued in the chapter "Thermidor in the Family" that the regressive policies on women and the family were a litmus test of the Stalinist degeneration of the Russian Revolution.

Hilary Wainwright is a British socialist and feminist. Her books include *The Lucas Plan: A New Trades Unionism in the Making?* (1981) (co-authored with David Elliott) and *Beyond the Fragments: Feminism and the Making of Socialism* (1980) (co-authored with Sheila Rowbotham and Lynne Segal). She is also the editor of the magazine *Red Pepper*.

Monique Wittig (1935–2003) was a French novelist and feminist theorist who wrote about overcoming socially enforced gender roles and who coined the phrase "heterosexual contract". She published her first novel, *L'Opponax* in 1964. Her second novel, *Les Guérillères* (1969) is better-known. Her 1980 paper "One is not Born a Woman" rejects the definition of lesbians as women because the word woman is constructed by sexist society.

Mary Wollstonecraft (1759–1797) was a British writer, philosopher, and advocate of women's rights. Her pioneering book *A Vindication of the Rights of Women* (1792) is one of the earliest feminist works. She was a central figure in the group of English intellectuals influenced by the ideas of the French Revolution, such as Thomas Paine and William Godwin – whom she married.

Iris Young (1949–2006) was Professor of Political Science at the University of Chicago, and affiliated with the Center for Gender Studies and the Human Rights programme there. She wrote a number of books on feminism and philosophy. She also engaged in a debate with both Nancy Fraser and Heidi Hartman, in two articles: "Beyond the Unhappy Marriage: a Critique of the Dual Systems Theory" and "Unruly Categories: a Critique of Nancy Fraser's Dual System Theory" in *New Left Review*. She wrote a number of books including *Justice and the Politics of Difference* (1990).

Mao Zedong (1893–1976) was a Chinese revolutionary communist writer and thinker. The Chinese revolution took place under his leadership in 1948-9. He placed more emphasis on the role of the peasantry than most other leaders.

Clara Zetkin (1857–1933) was a German Marxist theorist and activist like her close friend Rosa Luxemburg, first in the Social Democratic Party of Germany, then the Independent Social Democratic Party of Germany (USPD) and its far-left wing, the Spartacus League. This later became the Communist Party of Germany (KPD), which she represented in the Reichstag during the Weimar Republic from 1920 to 1933. She was heavily engaged in work for women's rights, editing from 1891 to 1917 the newspaper *Die Arbeiterin* or Working Woman, which changed its name in 1892 to *Die Gleichheit* or Equality. In 1910, she called for the establishment of International Women's Day, first celebrated on March 8, 1911.

Suggestions for further reading

On the historical links between the women's movement and labour movement:

Tony Cliff, *Class Struggle and Women's Liberation*, Bookmarks London, 1984.

Barbara Drake, *Women and Trade Unions*, Allen and Unwin, London, 1920.

Barbara Evans Clements, *Bolshevik Women*, Cambridge University Press, Cambridge, 1997.

Elizabeth Gurley Flynn, *I Speak My Own Piece: Autobiography of the "Rebel Girl"*, Masses and Mainstream, 1955.

Jill Liddington, Jill Norris, *One Hand Tied Behind Us: the rise of the women's suffrage movement*, Virago Press, London 1978.

Annik Mahaim, Alix Holt, Jacqueline Heinen, *Femmes et mouvement ouvrier*, La Breche, Paris 1979, (deals with three historical experiences: German Social democracy, the Russian revolution and the Spanish civil war).

Sylvia Pankhurst, *The Suffragette Movement*, Longman, London 1931, with foreword by Richard Pankhurst Virago, London 1977.

Cathy Porter, *Fathers and Daughters: Russian Women in Revolution*, Virago, London, 1976.

Sheila Rowbotham, *Women, Resistance and Revolution*, Allen Lane, 1973.

Barbara Taylor, *Eve and the New Jerusalem*, Virago, London, 1983.

Some essential classics (other editions will be available):

Simone de Beauvoir, *The Second Sex*, Everyman's Library, 1993.

Friedrich Engels, *The Origin of the Family, Private Property and the State*, Penguin Classics, London 2010.

Betty Friedan, *The Feminine Mystique*, Penguin Classics, London 2010.

Alexandra Kollontai, *Selected Writings,* W W Norton and company, New York & London, 1980.

Flora Tristan, *Peregrinations of a Pariah 1833-1834,* Beacon, Boston, 1987.

Mary Wollstonecraft, *A Vindication of the Rights of Woman and A Vindication of the Rights of Men,* Ed. Sylvana Tomaselli, Cambridge University Press, Cambridge, 1995.

Clara Zetkin, *Lenin on the Woman Question,* Literary Licensing, LLC (15 Oct 2011), *Selected Writings,* International Publishers Co Inc., US 1987 and articles available online at http://www.marxists.org/archive/zetkin/index.htm

From the second wave of the women's movement

On the origins of women's oppression:

Evelyn Reed, *Woman's Evolution: From Matriarchal Clan to Patriarchal Family,* Pathfinder Press, New York, 1975.

Eleanor Burke Leacock, *Myths of Male Dominance,* Monthly Review Press, New York, 1981.

Stephanie Coontz and Peta Henderson (ed.), *Women's Work, Men's Property: The Origins of Gender and Class,* Verso, London & New York, 1986.

On Psychology

Juliet Mitchell, *Psychoanalysis and Feminism,* Pantheon, New York, 1975.

Eli Zaretsky, *Capitalism, the Family and Personal Life,* Harper Pocketbooks, 1976.

The left and feminism

Arturo Peregalli, "PCI 1946-1970. Donna, famiglia, morale sessuale", *Quaderni Pietro Tresso,* n. 27, January-February 2001.

Sheila Rowbotham, Lynne Segal, Hilary Wainwright, *Beyond the Fragments: Feminism and the Making of Socialism,* The Merlin Press, London, 1979 (to be republished by Merlin Press in 2013).

Josette Trat, "L'histoire du courant 'féministe lutte de classe'", in *Femmes, genre, féminisme,* Syllepse, Paris 2007.

Lidia Cirillo, "Feminism of the Anti-Capitalist Left" in *International Viewpoint Online Magazine*, August, 2007.

Penelope Duggan (ed) *Women's Liberation & Socialist Revolution: Documents of the Fourth International*, Resistance Books & IIRE, London, 2011.

On the American feminist movement and black power:

Bell Hooks, *Ain't I a Woman: Black Women and Feminism*, South End Press, Boston, 1971.

Angela Davis, *Women, Race, and Class*, New York 1981.

Dayo Gore, Jeanne Theoharis, Komozi Woodard (eds.), *Want to Start a Revolution? Radical Women in the Black Freedom Struggle*, New York University Press New York – London 2009.

Reference works for radical feminism:

Shulamith Firestone, *The Dialectic of Sex: the Case for Feminist Revolution*, Farrar Straus Giroux, New York, 2003 (first published 1970).

Kate Millet, *Sexual Politics*, Doubleday, New York, 1970.

On feminist workerism/wages for housework and post-workerist feminism:

Maria Dalla Costa, Selma James, *The Power of Women & the Subversion of Community*, Wages for Housework Publisher, London, 1975.

Alisa del Re, "Produzione/riproduzione", in *Lessico marxiano*, Manifestolibri, Rome 2008, pp. 137-153.

On materialist feminism:

Christine Delphy, *Close to Home: Materialist Analysis of Women's Oppression*, University of Massachusetts Press, Boston 1984.

R. Hennessy and C. Ingraham (eds.), *Materialist Feminism. A Reader in Class, Difference and Women's Lives*, Routledge, New York and London 1997.

On lesbian feminism influenced by materialist feminism:

Monique Wittig, *The straight mind and other essays*, Beacon Press, Boston 1992.

On difference theory:

Luce Irigaray, *Speculum of the Other Woman*, Ithaca, 1985.

For a critique of this theory see Lidia Cirillo, *Lettera alle romane 2001* and in English *International Viewpoint Online Magazine* "For Another Difference".

On intersectionality:

Patricia Hill Collins and Margaret Andersen (eds.), *Race, Class and Gender: An Anthology*, Wadsworth Publishing, Belmont 1992.

E. Dorlin (ed.), *Sexe, race et classe. Pour une épistémologie de la domination*, PUF, Paris, 2009.

On queer theory:

Judith Butler, *Gender Trouble*, Routledge, New York 1990 and *Bodies that Matter*, Routledge, New York 1993.

Kevin Floyd, *The Reification of Desire. Toward a Queer Marxism*, University of Minnesota Press, Minneapolis 2009.

Recent debates:

Johanna Brenner – Maria Ramas, "Rethinking Women's Oppression", *New Left Review*, I/144 (1984);

Michèle Barret "Rethinking Women's Oppression: A Reply to Brenner and Ramas", *New Left Review*, I/146 (1984);

Nancy Fraser, *Justice Interruptus*, Routledge, New York-London 1997;

Iris Young, "Unruly Categories: A critique of Nancy Fraser's Dual System Theory", *New Left Review*, I/227 (1997);

Judith Butler, "Merely Cultural", *New Left Review*, I/227 (1998)

Nancy Fraser, "Heterosexism, Misrecognition and Capitalism: A Response to Judith Butler", *New Left Review*, I/228 (1998),

Judith Butler in Nancy Fraser, *Adding Insult to Injury: Nancy Fraser Debates Her Critics* Verso, New York and London 2008.

Other readings on the relationship between class and gender, patriarchy and capitalism, and sexuality and late capitalism:

Pat and Hugh Armstrong, "Beyond Sexless Class and Classless Sex: Towards Feminist Marxism", *Studies in Political Economy*, 53 (1983).

Michèle Barrett, *Women's Oppression Today: Problems in Marxist Feminist Analysis*, Verso, London 1980.

Zillah R. Eisenstein, *Capitalist Patriarchy and the Case for Socialist Feminism*, 1978.

Silvia Federici, *Caliban and the Witch. Women, the Body and Primitive Accumulation*, Autonomedia, Brooklyn, 2004.

Germaine Greer, *The Female Eunuch*, Harper Perennial Modern Classics, 2006 (first published 1970).

Rosemary Hennessy, *Profit and Pleasure. Sexual Identities in Late Capitalism*, Routledge, New York and London, 2000.

Claude Meillassoux, *Maidens, Meal and Money: Capitalism and the Domestic Community*, Cambridge University Press, Cambridge, 1981.

Lydia Sargent (ed.), *Women and Revolution: a Discussion of the Unhappy Marriage of Marxism and Feminism*, South End Press, Boston, 1981.

Lise Vogel, *Marxism and the Oppression of Women. Towards a Unitary Theory*, Rutgers University Press, 1987.

About Resistance Books and the IIRE

Resistance Books

Resistance Books is the publishing arm of Socialist Resistance, a revolutionary Marxist organization which is the British section of the Fourth International. Resistance Books publishes books jointly with the International Institute for Research and Education in Amsterdam and independently.

Further information about Resistance Books, including a full list of titles currently available and how to purchase them, can be obtained at http://www.resistancebooks.org, or by writing to Resistance Books, PO Box 62732, London, SW2 9GQ.

Socialist Resistance is an organization active in the trade union movement and in many campaigns against imperialist intervention in places like Afghanistan or Iraq, in solidarity with Palestine and with anti-capitalist movements across the globe. We are eco-socialist – we argue that much of what is produced under capitalism is socially useless and either redundant or directly harmful. Capitalism's drive for profit is creating environmental disaster – and it is the poor, the working class and people in the global south who are paying the highest price for this.

We have been long-standing supporters of women's liberation and the struggles of lesbians, gay people, bisexuals and transgender people. We believe these struggles must be led by those directly affected – none so fit to break the chains as those who wear them. We work in anti-racist and anti-fascist networks, including campaigns for the rights of immigrants and asylum seekers.

Socialist Resistance believes that democracy is an essential component of any successful movement of resistance and struggle. With Britain and the western imperialist countries moving into a long period of capitalist austerity and crisis, deeper than any since the Second World War, Socialist Resistance stands together with all those who are organizing to make another world possible.

Socialist Resistance is the bi-monthly magazine of the organization, which can be read online at www.socialistresistance. org. Socialist Resistance can be contacted by email at contact@ socialistresistance.org or by post at PO Box 62732, London, SW2 9GQ.

International Viewpoint is the English language online magazine of the Fourth International which can be read online at www.internationalviewpoint.org.

The International Institute for Research and Education

The International Institute for Research and Education (IIRE) is an international foundation, recognized in Belgium as an international scientific association by a Royal decree of 11th June 1981. The IIRE provides activists and scholars worldwide with opportunities for research and education in three locations: Amsterdam, Islamabad and Manila.

Since 1982, when the Institute opened in Amsterdam, its main activity has been the organization of courses in the service of progressive forces around the world. Our seminars and study groups deal with all subjects related to the emancipation of the world's oppressed and exploited. It has welcomed hundreds of participants from every inhabited continent. Most participants have come from the Third World.

The IIRE has become a prominent centre for the development of critical thought and interaction, and the exchange of experiences, between people who are engaged in daily struggles on the ground. The Institute's sessions give participants a unique opportunity to step aside from the pressure of daily activism. The IIRE gives them time to study, reflect upon their involvement in a changing world and exchange ideas with people from other countries.

Our website is constantly being expanded and updated with

freely downloadable publications, in several languages, and audio files. Recordings of several recent lectures given at the institute can be downloaded from www.iire.org - as can talks given by founding Fellows such as Ernest Mandel and Livio Maitan, dating back to the early 1980s.

The IIRE publishes *Notebooks for Study and Research* to focus on themes of contemporary debate or historical or theoretical importance. Lectures and study materials given in sessions in our Institute, located in Amsterdam, Manila and Islamabad, are made available to the public in large part through the Notebooks.

Different issues of the Notebooks have also appeared in languages besides English and French, including German, Dutch, Arabic, Spanish, Japanese, Korean, Portuguese, Turkish, Swedish, Danish and Russian.

For a full list of the *Notebooks for Study and Research,* visit http://bit.ly/IIRENSR or subscribe online at: http://bit.ly/NSRsub. To order the *Notebooks,* email iire@iire.org or write to International Institute for Research and Education, Lombokstraat 40, Amsterdam, NL-1094.